NICOLE PIEROTTI

No More Nappies!

A STEP BY STEP GUIDE TO TOILET TRAINING YOUR TODDLER

Nicole Pierotti, child psychologist and mum of three, will help busy parents get through toilet training with ease!

Nicole Pierotti

**No More Nappies!
A Step By Step Guide To Toilet
Training Your Toddler**

This edition first published in 2016 in Australia.

Copyright © 2016 Nicole Pierotti

The author asserts her moral rights in this work throughout the world without waiver. All rights reserved. No part of this publication may be reproduced, stored in a retrieval system or transmitted in any form or by any means (electronic or mechanical, through reprography, digital transmission, recording or otherwise) without the prior written permission of the publisher.

National Library of Australia Cataloguing-in-Publication entry
Pierotti, Nicole.
No More Nappies! A Step By Step Guide To Toilet
Training Your Toddler

ISBN 978-0-9872533-3-0
Edited by Brendan Pierotti & Karen Torrisi
Photographs by Jennifer Gilchrist Photography

Disclaimers - While every care has been taken in researching and compiling the information in this book, it is in no way intended to replace specific professional medical advice and counselling for you and your toddler. Parents are encouraged to seek such help, as they deem necessary. The author and publisher specifically disclaim any liability arising from the application of information in this book. Every effort has been made to obtain permission to reproduce material from other sources. Where permission could not be obtained, the publisher welcomes hearing from the copyright holder(s) in order to acknowledge that copyright.

For information on other Babysmiles titles, www.babysmiles.com.au

This is Isabella, she will show you how to go Nappy free...

To the many wonderful parents whom I've had the privilege to work with over the years and who have 'asked' me many times for this book

To Karen for your persistent reminders to keep writing.

ABOUT THE AUTHOR

Nicole Pierotti combines academic smarts with maternal wisdom to help parents conquer the challenges they face when raising babies and small children. A psychologist for over 24 years, Nicole has specialised in baby sleep and child behaviour for the past 15. With three children of her own, she is well accustomed to the struggles that frequently drive parents crazy! Readers and clients easily relate to Nicole and find her methods not just incredibly insightful but also sanity-saving. Nicole's website www.babysmiles.com.au is a treasure trove of information accessible 24/7 ... perfect, considering parenthood itself is a 24/7 commitment.

CONTENTS

Easy Toilet Training 10
What You Need to Know to Start....................................... 11
Is my Child Ready?... 12
Your Attitude.. 15
Age.. 16
How Long Should It Take?.. 16
Day Control... 16
Night Control.. 17
How to make the Switch from Nappy to Toilet............... 18

Pre-Toilet Training 20
The Start of Teaching your Toddler.................................... 20
Your Toddler's Clues that They are Getting Ready........ 23
Signs Your Toddler is Ready... 23
Signs that You the Parent are Ready................................ 26

It's Time To Start – How To Toilet Train 27
Ideas to make it Easy - Toilet Training Tips.................... 29
Equipment... 30
Toilet or Potty?
Pros and Cons of Toilet Choices 39
Do I need Training Pants?.. 41
Clothing... 45
Potty Words 46

Nicole's Six Steps to Easy Toilet Training 48

Step 1   Learn by Watching You 52
Step 2   Play and Read 54
Step 3   Tell them what You are Expecting 60
Step 4   Starting to Learn and Practice 61
Step 5   Praise and Encouragement 78
Step 6   Prompts 86
Accidents 86
Tips for Boys 88
Do's and Don'ts of Toilet Training 89

Common Questions – Expert Answers 91

Asking too late 91
Constipation 92
Daycare and Babysitters 93
Don't Flush it, it's mine! 95
Fear 95
Going backwards – Regression 96
Going outside 101
He has tantrums whenever I ask him to sit and try 102
I need you 103
I will make you 105
In the car 105
I've tried everything 106
Moving from potty to toilet 109
My potty and only mine! 112
Night control 114
Professional help 117
Punishment 118

Save it for the nappy 119
Smearing 120
Sticky bottoms 120
Trying every toilet 121
Where's the toilet? Out and About 123
Working mums and dads 124

Ask Nicole 125

Dads and daughters in public bathrooms 125
Fear of flushing 126
Shocked at their own poo 127
Stalling bedtime with toilet visits 128
Touching his penis on the potty 129

Support 130

Online packages and support 130
Signs your Toddler is Ready to Toilet Train 133
Signs you a Parent are Ready to Toilet Train
 your Toddler 135
Professional help 140
Acknowledgements 141

Nicole's Tip:

Throughout this book you will see the above symbol. This shows where I have added advice that I have found works well through workshops with many families. They are the essential points for you to focus on. Read these carefully.

Easy Toilet Training

WHAT YOU NEED TO KNOW TO START

So, you're starting to wonder if your toddler is ready to start learning to use the toilet during the day. Where to from here? How do I go about starting? What do I need? Are they too young? Firstly, let us just keep it simple.

Toilet training is a natural process and meant to be simple. However, it can get quite complicated the more you read and talk to other mothers. Let's get back to basics.

Nicole's Tip:

It is a natural bodily process – what goes in must come out. First of all, you need to get over any embarrassment that you have about this process before you can start to teach your child.

Just as you use the toilet without thinking about it, your toddler uses their nappy without thinking about it. Toilet training is all about your toddler noticing what their body is doing. Then being able to tell you what is happening. Then finally being able to control and hold that urge until they get to the toilet.

It takes time, patience, practice, praise and more patience. It will not be done in a day or a week. More likely it will take months.

A lot of parents expect toilet training to be long and difficult. In reality, a lot of difficulties can be prevented or minimised if you wait until your child is ready and then you go about training in a logical, consistent and matter-of-fact way.

> Your child must be ready.
>
> How do you know if they are ready? Well, there is a difference between your toddler starting to notice that they are doing a poo or a wee and being at the right place to be able to learn to control this function.
>
> Let's have a better look at this point.

Isabella in her pull-up

IS MY CHILD READY?

Before we start, let me say that many parents can't avoid comparing their child to other children. They feel disappointed if their child doesn't do something as early as other children. They feel proud if they do it early. It seems that parents sometimes forget that it's not a competition. They may even look at what age their child is when they learn to do something as a direct reflection of their own parenting abilities.

Just because a child is a certain age doesn't mean automatically that they are ready.

Nicole's Tip:

The development or readiness that you are looking for gradually happens over a few months. Most children are ready between 18 months and 3 years of age.

By developmental readiness I mean their body is ready in two ways: physically and emotionally. Firstly, (physically) their body is able to give them signals that they have a wee or a poo coming. Secondly, (emotionally) they are keen to learn and willing to move to this next stage. Developmentally, both of these stages of readiness are more likely to be between 2 to 3 years of age.

If in doubt please WAIT......

Why? Starting too early can lead to a lack of motivation in your child. They can stop and start, you too can lose your enthusiasm and it can take a long, long time.

If it is at the right time it will only take weeks to months.

AVOID starting because

- ☒ Grandma is pressuring you to
- ☒ All your friends are doing it
- ☒ It's holiday time
- ☒ You have pressure from childcare to do so
- ☒ You want to save money on nappies
- ☒ You are over the nappy changes and cleaning up
- ☒ This is the age you were toilet trained

It's best WHEN

- ☑ Your child is interested in the toilet
- ☑ The weather is warm
- ☑ There are NO major changes in your life – Not moving house
- ☑ Not having another baby

- ☑ Grandma isn't visiting
- ☑ Dad isn't working away
- ☑ Your child notices before, during or after the fact that a poo or wee is coming out
- ☑ Your child is keen and WANTS to become independent.... If they are not interested it is impossible to toilet train
- ☑ Your child lets you know that they are wet or have done a poo in their nappy
- ☑ Your child asks to go to the toilet

The science of our plumbing:

Which comes first, Bladder control or Bowel control?

Remember back to those early baby days where there were multiple poos a day and many nappy changes? As your baby grew, their bowel movements moved into a pattern. They were more predictable and there were less of them a day.

Next, bowel control develops (toddlers can hold onto those poos). Then daytime bladder control happens (they are able to hold those wees).

Finally, lastly and sometime later, children are able to control their nighttime bladder. Holding onto those wees all night can be rather difficult.

YOUR ATTITUDE

Once your toddler is ready for toilet training it should be a SIMPLE and SMOOTH process; it is essential that you have a relaxed and unpressured attitude to toilet training. I know we all get frustrated at times for cleaning up the wee yet again, however, do not ever let your toddler hear, see or feel your frustration. Just keep it relaxed.

Things go wrong when there is too much pressure, mum is stressed or in a hurry for this to happen and it all starts to backfire.

♥ Keep it positive with lots and lots of praise, keep it natural and keep it non-threatening to your child.

Bella and her mum with lots of praise

AGE

Remember that the most common age is from 18 months to 3 years. It is not a competition and certainly not a sign of your child's intelligence if they are ready early or later. It's also not a measure of your success at parenting. It's all to do with them, their body and their readiness.

 Nicole's Tip:

Get it wrong and start too early – then you end up putting more pressure on your toddler and the whole process of training will take a year or longer.

Children will resist if it is too early.

HOW LONG SHOULD IT TAKE?

That depends, but the promises of 'toilet train in a day' or 'toilet train in a week' are outside the norm.

Expect several weeks to several months to be confident and to know that your child is toilet trained fully.

Some children are ready early and when they train it can be very quick; for others it is a fair bit longer.

DAY CONTROL

Day control comes way before night control. They are two separate training scenarios. Bowel control usually comes before Bladder control, though it doesn't always. It is much easier – as you can appreciate – for a toddler to hold onto a poo than a wee. The wee kind of just comes out with very little warning; whereas with a poo they are able to hold on a little and let you know when they are doing one. You also can generally tell when a poo is starting or on its way.

A good time to watch your child is usually within 20–30 minutes or so of eating, as it is a common time for them to need to go to the toilet. You can tell from the expression on their face, their stance (squatting/keeping still/straining), or sound effects they make.

FACT: 98% of children are daytime trained by the age of 4 years.

FACT: Most toddlers wee 4–8 times a day, about every 2 hours or so.

FACT: Most toddlers have 1 or 2 poos a day though sometimes they skip a day.

NIGHT CONTROL

Being dry at night is a separate stage to toilet training and comes quite some time after day control. A general guide I give parents is that it tends to happen about a year later than day control. So don't be too quick to cross those nappies or pull-ups off your grocery list. It is normal for some children at 4-5 years of age to occasionally wet the bed at night. Night dryness has a window of opportunity that you need to look for, notice and then act on. Basically, don't even try night training until you notice that your child's nappy is dry for several nights in a row. At that point, ditch the nappy or pull-ups and go straight to knickers or jocks. More about this later in the book.

A word of warning here about the window of opportunity: it has been my experience with parents that children are keen and motivated during this time. But if you keep going with the nappies and pull ups because it's convenient for you or 'just in case' then the motivation of your child wanes and they then become reliant on the nappy or pull up and the window is missed. They get the 'oh well it doesn't matter' attitude. It then typically takes years for that motivation to return.

FACT: Day toilet training has nothing to do with night time dryness.

FACT: Night dryness only happens when your child's physiology supports it. It involves the kidneys, brain and bladder. You can't teach it. You can't rush it.

HOW TO MAKE THE SWITCH FROM NAPPY TO TOILET

So what's next? It's a great idea to start with a bit of 'setting the scene'. By this I mean, let's start some informal training and education. You will probably naturally do this or may have already been doing this. Get over your shyness of your bodily functions, stop closing the door when you go to the toilet and invite your toddler in... Remember: what goes in must come out!

Start to implement all the ideas in this next section a couple of months before actually starting toilet training formally. You may find reading through this that you are already doing all or most of these without thinking. If so, great!

It is a natural process so keep moving forward.

Pre-Toilet Training

THE START OF TEACHING YOUR TODDLER

Your Demo Bring your child with you when you go to the toilet. Talk about what is happening. It is not a science lesson, just chat about what you are doing as you go.

Tell him, 'This is where the poos and wees go' and 'Mummy and Daddy don't wear nappies but use the toilet.' Explain about wiping, let him look in the toilet after you have finished to see the evidence and let him flush the toilet. If he doesn't want to flush, this is fine.

♥ Explain what it feels like to want to go to the toilet. Talk about that feeling low down in your tummy-bottom, point to his tummy-bottom. Try to make the connection between the feeling and going.

♥ Get him to notice and tell you when he wets or soils his nappy. Then take him and his nappy down to the toilet and tip it into the toilet as best you can, explaining this is where it goes. Get him to flush it away.

♥ If he's told you in the lounge that he's done a poo, still go to the toilet and empty the poo into the toilet (if possible). Keep a packet of flushable wipes stored in the toilet and continue to wipe and clean up here. You can then flush the wipes away.

♪ Start teaching hygiene by introducing the concept of hand washing afterwards. Make it fun. Sing a song if you like. "This is how we wash our hands, wash our hands, wash our hands..."

♥ Encourage your child to do things on their own like pulling their pants up. Part of toilet training involves being able to pull down their pants quickly!

♥ When eating meals keep making those connections between food and drink going into their body, their body taking what it needs and the leftover food coming out as poo. The wee is your leftover drink. They usually quite enjoy this fact and may tell everyone they know!

☺ It's also a great idea to look at a picture that talks about food going in and coming out or to draw one yourself whenever doing some art and craft. Your toddler loves to learn!

☺ Check and change your language if you need to: I hear a lot of parents make comments about their baby's or toddler's dirty nappy and use words and phrases such as 'stinky', 'yuck', 'that's so bad' and 'that's disgusting'. This gives doing a poo a bad image and little children pick up on this. If you use language like this, now is the time to change; we want doing a poo to be a good thing!

♥ Read a story book about learning to use the potty; there are a number of good ones about. You can buy a book or visit your local library and chat to the librarians who will no doubt point you in the right direction. Have a look at our online shop at www.babysmiles.com.au/shop

♥ Now is also the time to talk about 'wet' and 'dry'. If your toddler hasn't worked out the meanings of these two words by about 14 months or so, start to point out and talk about wet and dry. Are your hands wet? Are they dry? Let's get dry, after a bath. You are wet getting out of the bath. Use this wherever you notice wet and dry, this will help later for wet and dry pants.

Still wondering if it's too early? If in doubt, WAIT a month or two and read this again.

Part of toilet training involves being able to pull their pants down quickly!

YOUR TODDLER'S CLUES THAT THEY ARE GETTING READY

Checklist…

Most toddlers begin to give you clues that they are getting ready for toilet training. The signs or clues can be seen from 18 months onwards but mostly occur from 24–30 months (2 yrs – 2 ½ yrs).

I like to look for three different areas of Readiness with Children.

1. Physical Readiness: is your toddler's body giving you and them clues that they are able to hold on?

2. Emotional Readiness: is your toddler ready and keen to start?

3. General Readiness: there are some basic things that your child should be able to do. To help keep the training smooth, let's not make it too hard for them.

SIGNS THAT YOUR TODDLER IS READY

Child Readiness Checklist

- ☑ She can be dry for a couple of hours at a time
- ☑ She wees a fair amount of liquid in one go, not just tiny little bits

- ☑ Her poos are regular and you can see a pattern in the time of day she does them

- ☑ She notices or gives you a clue that she is doing a poo or wee – usually toddlers stop what they are doing, crouch down or bend their knees, clutch their nappy area or sometimes they even go and hide when doing a wee

- ☑ She simply tells you or asks to be changed after she has done a wee or poo

- ☑ She is keen to wear underwear or training pants

- ☑ She may look for a little privacy when doing a wee or poo

- ☑ She is able to follow simple directions like 'sit down' and 'quick, let's go!'

- ☑ She wants to co-operate with mum's instructions

- ☑ She can walk well (she needs to actually be able to get to the toilet in a hurry)

- ☑ She can pull her pants up and down. Try to make it easy with clothing that is easy to remove while training; no need to make it trickier than it is!

- ☑ She has a basic understanding of what the toilet is for

- ☑ She wants to please mum or dad. She is not in the difficult 'no' stage (when they want to see what you will do about it…) You don't need any battles about toilet training!

- ☑ She can sit quietly for short periods of time. For example, 5–10 minutes to do a puzzle, read a book, because she will need to do so on the potty
- ☑ She notices or can tell you that she is doing a wee

You don't need every one of these points on the readiness checklist to be present but your toddler needs MOST of the points to be ticked. The more that are there, the more successful toilet training will be for both of you.

 Nicole's Tip:

If your child isn't 'ready' then it can be frustrating and discouraging. If in doubt, WAIT a little longer, read this list and think about it again. I suggest waiting 8 weeks before trying again.

Can sit quietly for short periods of time

SIGNS THAT YOU – 'THE PARENT' – ARE READY

Your child is ready now but what about you?

When you are teaching your child anything, especially toilet training, you as the parent must be willing to do this. Be patient but keen to move onto the next stage. Positive, positive and more positive...

⭐ If you are going through a difficult time, feel impatient with your child, are easily frustrated and/or very tired then this is not the right time to start toilet training.

Toilet training is not done in a day, no matter the promises you've heard. It is usually weeks and then months before you are confident that your child is day trained.

Your job as a parent is like a coach. You need to help, remind, be patient, teach new skills, clean up accidents without reprimand, wash dirty clothes, change clothes, help your toddler run to the toilet at a moment's notice, drop everything you are doing immediately and take your toddler to the toilet, all the while being positive and encouraging them to hold on!

Make no mistake that this process can be frustrating at times and accidents will happen without a doubt. If you prepare yourself and know how to approach this, pull-ups will soon be a thing of the past.

PARENT READINESS CHECKLIST

- ☐ Am I positive?
- ☐ Do I have time?
- ☐ Am I getting enough sleep?
- ☐ Am I patient?
- ☐ Do I have all the things I need?
- ☐ Is this the right time for our family?

So your child is all set and so are you now, with a positive attitude and enthusiasm at the ready. Well then, it's time...

Adapted from Janet Hall 1995

It's Time To Start – How To Toilet Train

Just remember: *It's harder than you think*

For your child to learn to use a toilet here's an outline of what's involved. Perhaps it's harder than you think. Just like learning to walk, there will be mishaps, stumbles, successes and cheers. Above all it will take time, practice and patience. However, your child will get there in the end.

You will be the teacher and your child is going to learn what to do with the potty and how to hold on to their wee and poo.

Here's a summary of what you are going to teach and what your child has to learn…

- Know what it feels like to have to 'go'
- Not use his nappy despite automatically doing this for years
- Stop what he's doing and tense the muscle holding the bladder/anus
- Work out in his brain where the toilet is and to hold on
- Say that he needs to go to someone
- Walk/run to the toilet or potty, *whilst* holding on
- Pull down his pants, *whilst* still holding on when his body is saying 'hurry up, I need to go!'
- Sit down and relax, wait – relax the muscles and then release what's there
- Be patient and wait 'til he's finished – that's a relief!
- Wipe, don't use too much paper! Count the squares
- Get off the toilet
- Pull up his pants
- Flush
- Go to the sink, wash and dry his hands
- Be keen to do this many, many times a day

All the steps your child needs to learn

IDEAS TO MAKE IT EASY... TRAINING TIPS

So where to go from here? Gather everything you need (which isn't much) and then simply make a day to start and tell your child you are starting.

EQUIPMENT

It's pretty simple, or well it should be. All you need is

- A potty
- A portable potty/or cushioned seat
- Some training pants
- One keen toddler
- A positive, patient parent

One of the first decisions you need to make is do you use the potty – the little chair type which you place on the floor in the toilet room, or do you get the potty seat that fits over the regular toilet seat?

A plain and simple potty

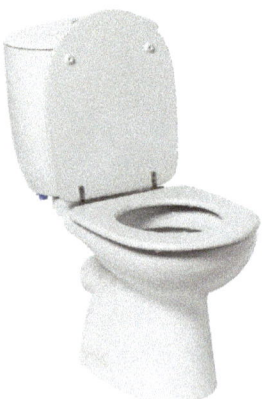

An Adult size Toilet

Nicole's Tip: Potty

Let me sway you this way. It makes sense to start out with a potty and the toilet is rather large and can be daunting for lots of kids.

It also takes a lot of effort to actually get up there – it can be quite scary having their legs dangling, not to mention the threat of falling in. However, this is certainly your end goal. Obviously, the quicker you can get to the big toilet the easier the clean up is. Flush and you're done. With a potty, you need to empty and then clean.

There are more steps in the process. It's like going straight from a baby's bottle to a cup and skipping the sipper cup step if your toddler doesn't like sipper cups.

⭐ If your child is keen for the big toilet, there is no reason why you can't skip the potty step and go straight there. Just be sure to make it easy to access, make sure there is a stool and practice getting on and off the toilet. They need a stool to help them climb up and it certainly is better to place their feet flat onto a stool or step when pushing out a poo.

Isla (22 months) on the big toilet enjoying a magazine

In reality, most children like the potty as it's less intimidating and they can sit there while you are on the toilet. They find this much easier to get on and off and are not worried about climbing. This makes it easier to move onto the toilet. The more independent they are, the better, as you may not always be urgently available every time they need to go. Independence is the goal.

Be sure the stair type models are really, really sturdy and not wobbly in any way. Wobbly stairs will make for a scary experience for your toddler and you do not need that!

A ladder example to help your toddler climb to a toilet

A Step stool to make reaching easier

★ Take your toddler with you when you buy the potty, test out the most stable and comfortable potties. (When you come home, explain what it's for, he can practice sitting with his clothes on if he wants to.)

Here comes the next dilemma: you've decided on the potty option, now which one do you buy? If you've had a look around it can be quite daunting. There is the plain and simple $10 potty all the way up to the musical, padded throne fitted with flashing lights for $100.

Nicole's Tip:

I think potties should be plain and simple. They are not toys. It's just a little portable toilet until your child goes to the big toilet.

I find that if your potty resembles a toilet the transition is better and it also helps when out and about and using other toilets that they are all similar versions not vastly different to the throne at home.

So keep it simple.

My Tip: keep pottie's simple

⭐ I would recommend buying a potty that is stable for your child. Get one that isn't easily going to wriggle or tip as they move around.

Also, keep in mind how easy it will be to clean. If it has an insert where the wee and poo is collected, that is easy to remove, can FIT and be tipped into the toilet. This is a far easier process of cleaning than lifting the whole potty.

One of many types of pottie's with a removable insert – definitely makes cleaning easier. Tip into the toilet and flush. I like this potty because it has a high back and sides and is very sturdy.

Nicole's Tip:

Keep the potty in the toilet, not in front of the TV, or in the back yard. It's a bit of a rush the first week, but once your toddler has the idea and can hold for a little, they will get there to the toilet. Always think bigger than today, as your end aim is to teach your child to run to the toilet.

If you have a house with more than one level – definitely get two potties, one for downstairs and one for upstairs. Place them in the toilets. If you do not have two toilets then put them in a logical place.

Nicole's Tip:

Remember, you do not want to move them around and be looking frantically, trying to remember where you put the potty!

It's a good idea to buy a portable toilet or toilet seat insert, which basically converts any big toilet to a child size. Inserts can be padded and fold up usually in four and come with a little drawstring carry bag. This is great for when you are out and there are no kids' toilets in sight but most parenting rooms are usually designed to have a child size toilet.

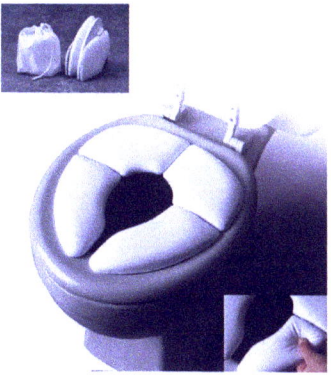

I love this portable toilet seat insert, it folds in quarters and is very portable for use anywhere. You can even pop it in the bottom of your pram to use on toilets out n about

Miley and her portable potty – Portable-potty comes with reusable insert with disposable one-time use inserts. The choice is yours

PROS AND CONS OF TOILET CHOICES

A Potty

- ☑ Small, and easy for your toddler to sit on
- ☑ Not scary, non-threatening
- ☑ Your toddler can easily put their feet flat onto the floor
- ☑ Portable if needed
- ☑ Stable so your toddler won't fall in
- ☑ Your toddler doesn't need your help to get onto it
- ☒ You need to empty, rinse and clean after each use
- ☒ You may have to take it with you if they become so used to the potty they won't use other toilets
- ☒ You need to buy one or two if you have another bathroom
- ☒ Your toddler will need to move to a toilet later

Plain and simple potty (Recommended)

Other type of Pottie's

A TOILET SEAT INSERT (GOES ON THE BIG TOILET)

- ☑ No cleaning, just flush away with the press of a button
- ☑ When you move to a toilet, it's very simple just remove the insert off the toilet,
no change
- ☑ Portable if needed
- ☑ This is where your toddler needs to end up anyway so you skip a step and keep it simpler
- ☑ No potty on the bathroom floor
- ☒ It can be scary for your toddler to climb up
- ☒ Your toddler may feel that they may fall in, though unlikely
- ☒ You need to buy one or two if you have another bathroom
- ☒ Your toddler can't put their feet on the floor, you can add a high stool
- ☒ Your toddler may need your help to get up – not independent
- ☒ You will have to take the insert on and off when you use the toilet

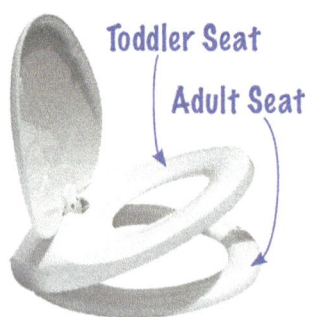

A fixed toilet seat that has a toddler seat option to lift up or down

TOILET

- ☑ No cleaning, just flush
- ☑ Your toddler needs to end up here anyway so you can skip all the previous steps
- ☑ No adjustment for your toddler from potty to toilet
- ☑ Don't need to buy anything
- ☑ Can use toilets everywhere
- ☒ It can be very scary for your toddler to climb up
- ☒ Your toddler may feel that they may fall in, you will need to hold them each time – not independent at all
- ☒ If they fall in once, they are likely to have a fear of the toilet
- ☒ Your toddler can't put their feet on the floor

Adapted from Pantley 2007

DO I NEED TRAINING PANTS?

Yes, this is a great idea, so get 10 terry towelling training pants because they are thicker than underwear. Training pants give your child a little more leeway when the wee starts coming out. With underwear such as jocks and knickers, the wee is not absorbed at all and runs down their legs in a second flat. They are also a bit stretchier when pulling up and down while your child is learning this skill.

Another big plus for training pants is that your child can feel being wet unlike a pull-up that pulls the moisture immediately away from the skin. This un-comfortableness is what you need to keep your child motivated and keen to recognise and tell you they need to go.

Training Pants

Just be careful not to purchase really thick training pants that look mostly like a nappy but with cloth, as these do not give the feeling of wetness, which is what is really important during toilet training.

There are many different types of training pants, look for cotton pants, not too thick but thicker than undies.

Though having said that, training pants are not a must. If you want to just go straight to knickers/jocks then do so.

You can take your child shopping for the training pants, talk about how they 'are for big kids' in a positive way and how soon he will be swapping his nappies for 'big kid pants' or 'training pants' while learning to use the toilet.

 Nicole's Tip:

Find a special spot to put them in the toilet/ bathroom. Show him how to put them on and off. Give lots and lots of praise, even if it's not quite right.

WHAT ABOUT PULL-UPS?

Once you decide to start training, off go the pull-ups, as they are not much different to nappies. Except for day sleeps and night time, use knickers, jocks or training pants. I would only use pull-ups if your child was undoing their nappy during sleep time or if you are shopping or driving long distances to get to town and the 1 second warning isn't enough! Pull-ups are then handy on the side of the road, to pull down like you would with pants. Alternatively, line the car seat with the disposable car seat liners. This will give you some peace of mind.

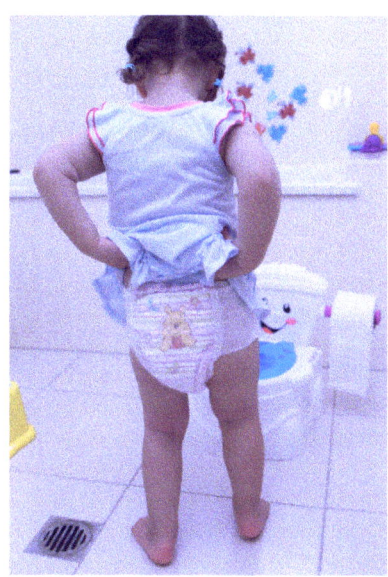

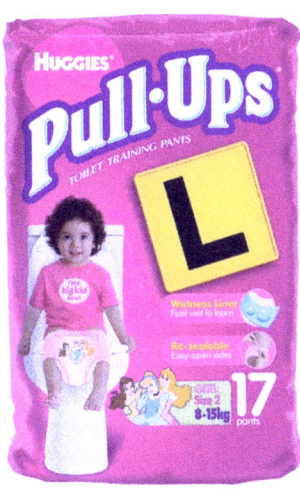

Most brands of nappies also make pull-ups or training pants

Nicole's Tip:

There are special liners available for car seats to help prevent the 'what if...' situation and a wet car seat. These are handy when you are fairly confident with your child's ability to hold on and tell you when they need to go.

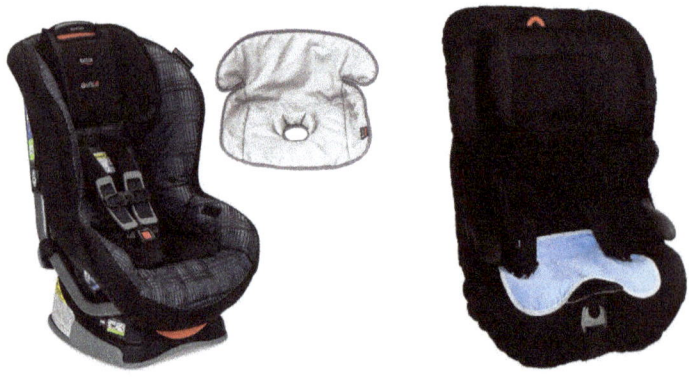

Car Seat waterproof liner & booster liners

It is certainly best to avoid using pull-ups as part of your training daily at home as you really want them to feel the difference between wet and dry. I know as a parent how hard it is to let go of that 'insurance' or 'peace of mind' that pull-ups/nappies bring. After all, you are assured of no accidents when they are wearing them.

The other problem parents often run into without realising it, is that you do not rush or run so fast if your toddler is wearing pull-ups as you have a backup...

CLOTHING

Please give some thought to the type of clothing you dress your child in every morning. The harder the clothing is to remove or pull down, the harder and less successful it will be for your little one to remove when they are in a mad rush and they are desperately trying to 'hold on'.

For girls, a summer dress is usually the easiest as they simply pull up (hopefully out of the way) and down go the knickers. For a boy, elastic waist pants which are rather comfortable and stretchy are easiest.

For the moment forget about complicated clothing such as overalls, buttons and zips. Summer is also a better time if possible, as there is certainly way less clothing to remove. As they become more practiced at removing clothing and holding on, you can have a wider choice once again.

If you have a girl, go with dresses for the moment or loose fitting pants. If you have a boy, make sure his pants are loose fitting and with elastic while training as being able to pull them down easily and quickly is very, very important.

Nicole's Tip:

When you start training for the first week just go with t-shirts and pants/jocks/knickers to make it easy for your toddler (weather permitting).

Keep it simple, t-shirts and knickers

POTTY WORDS

When it comes potty/toilet training you need to give some thought to the words you prefer or you are more likely to use. Having different names for body parts, toilets and urine can become quite confusing for toddlers. Here is a guide. Please read it, think and discuss with others living in your house and then choose the ones you prefer. Then stick to them! And get others to as well.

Nicole's Tip:

I recommend where possible choosing the 'real' name rather than slang names. There should be no embarrassment in calling a penis a 'penis' rather than a willy, pee pee, bits or any other such name. It is too confusing for children and private body parts have names just like your 'elbow', 'nose' does.

Be consistent with your wording so make sure you are not saying 'let's go the bathroom' one day, then the next 'let's do a tinkle' or do you have to 'wee'. Keep it simple.

 WHICH WORDS WILL YOU USE?

Toilet	**Toilet**, pot, potty, privy, loo
Urination	**Wee**, pee, pee-pee, go potty, tinkle, wee-wee, go number one, go to the bathroom, whistle, boy parts
Bowel Movement	**Poo**, poop, poo-poo, BM, go number two, go to the bathroom, caca, business
Penis	**Penis**, privates, willy, pee-pee
Vulva	Vulva, **vagina**, privates, girl parts
Bottom	**Bottom**, bum, buttocks, rectum, tush, cheeks, behind, rear

*My suggestions are in bold

Pantley 2007

Nicole's Six Steps to Easy Toilet Training

So you have everything you need, you've done your checklists and all that's left is to pick a day to start. Remember, it's a process that happens over weeks or months and won't be done in a day or a week.

As psychologists, we often research and educate others about learning especially in the way we learn best. In my six steps of toilet training I have purposely used different types of teaching and learning. If you follow the steps, you will have given your toddler a number of different ways to learn about toilet training.

The different forms of learning you will teach your toddler are:

Verbal	Talking
Modelling	Using a doll
Imitation	Watch you go to the toilet
Practice	Trying again and again
Praise	Clapping & Cheering
Rewards	Stickers, Prize boxes & charts
Prompting	Reminded by you & potty watch

Reading – using the doll and practising.

Let's get started and follow the six steps. The first three steps are learning steps that happen either months before or the week before your 'starting day'.

Step 1   **Learn by watching** Mummy and Daddy.
Open the door and let your toddler in when you go to the toilet and talk to them about everything that is going in the toilet.

Step 2   **Practice with their doll** over the next few days. Then pick the day to start. Saturdays are usually best if you are working. Also, remember to **read books** on toilet training.

Step 3   **Tell them what you are expecting.** A few days before potty training starts, talk to your toddler and explain that "in three days I am going to teach you how to use the potty." Make sure you are excited. Explain the steps you are going to do and how much fun it will be. This is a good time to take your toddler to the shops and buy some big boy underwear/or training pants and talk to them about how they will be able to wear them. If you haven't already bought your potty then do this now as well. Be excited and they will too!

Step 4 **Start practising!** On your start day and at the start of each day after, spend a few minutes practising a quick dash to the toilet. A pretend 'it's time to go'. Have your child practise running to the potty, pulling down their pants, sitting down and waiting. Add in lots of cheers and claps. Make this a game.

Stay close by, read a book about toilet training and then at timed intervals take your toddler to the potty and 'sit and try' and when there is success finally make sure you clap, sing, dance, high five.

At the start, success is really by chance until your toddler "gets it". Then – of course – they won't get it every time, but that's the practice bit.

After a few days, the best times to sit are after a meal (as the bowel is stimulated by a full stomach), after exercise or just after waking up.

Remember, no more nappies for day time except day sleeps and nighttime.

Nicole's Tip:

It may help to move to pull-ups at the day sleep times so that your child isn't really going back to nappies. As soon as those pull-ups are dry for three days in a row at day sleep time then remove them completely and use underwear.

Step 5   **Praise and Encouragement.** Rewards, Prize boxes and Sticker charts all keep toddlers interested. They love to mark their achievements on the chart and select prizes.

Step 6   **Prompts:** After the first few days move from reminders of "It's time to sit" to asking. Ask your child "Do you have to do a wee?" or "Do you have to do a poo?"

Before you head out the house to the shops, do a toilet practice and say 'let's go do a wee'. If your toddler adamantly tells you that they don't have to, patiently explain that 'we just try before we go.'

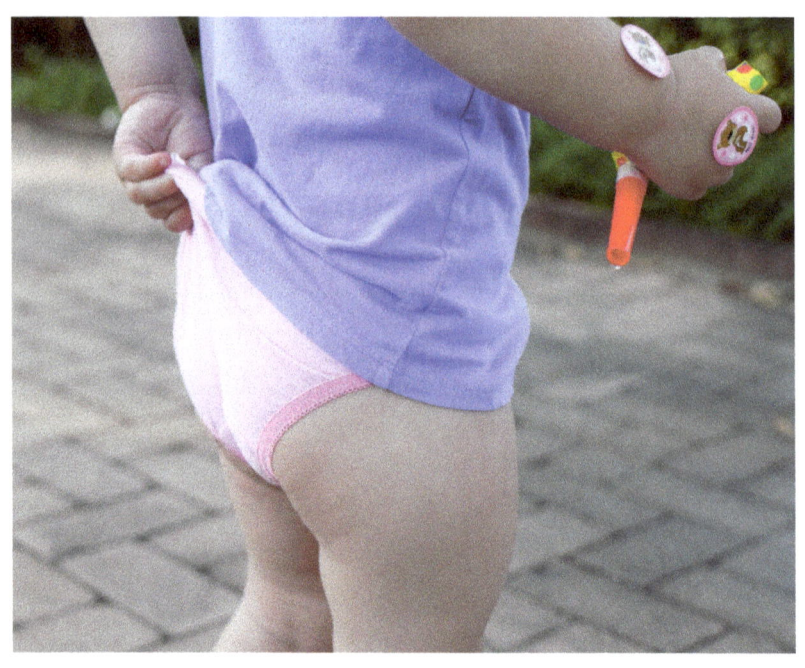

Try to avoid nappies during the day, save it for car trips or daytime sleeps.

STEP 1 LEARN BY WATCHING YOU

Bring your child with you when you go to the toilet. Talk about what is happening. It is not a science lesson, just chat about what you are doing as you go. Tell him 'this is where the poos and wees go' and 'Mummy and Daddy don't wear nappies but use the toilet.' Explain about wiping, let him look in the toilet after you have finished to see the evidence and let him flush the toilet. If he doesn't want to flush, this is fine.

Isabella copying after watching

STEP 2 PLAY AND READ

Practice-Play with their Doll

Children love to play. They play with dolls and toys and teddies. As they play, they act out all sorts of things that have happened in their day. So use this play to your advantage as another way to teach them about toilet training.

Simply start by sitting down with a doll or teddy and go through the steps of playing, noticing they have to go to the toilet – they can feel it in their bladder, quickly jumping up, running to the toilet while holding on, pulling their pants down, sitting down, letting it go or pushing it out.

Bella practice-playing with her doll

Nicole's Tip:

Be sure to note the difference between a poo and a wee. Poos take a bit of pushing and wees just come out fast!

Then it's time for them to wipe, flush, pull their pants back up and wash their hands. Select any toy your child plays with or you can buy a doll that wets (which essentially has a hole at the mouth and another at the bottom). You give them a drink and it wets out the other end. You can practise sitting them on the potty and showing your toddler what is expected. We learn by copying as well as doing.

Get your toddler to take the doll through the steps of going to the toilet: wiping, washing hands etc. As well, take a look at our online shop for products for toilet training at www.babysmiles.com.au/shop.

Of course, any favourite toy will do the trick as well and it doesn't need to be specially designed. A teddy or toy can sit on the potty and you can pour a little water into the potty to show 'pretend wees' and follow up with the flush, which you can make sound effects for.

Bella giving reward stickers to her doll

Nicole's Tip:

Using the doll with the other techniques is a great teaching tool as children love this type of play.

If you're not sure what to say, then try this.

DOLL PLAY – THE SCRIPT

When sitting down with your toddler's doll or teddy and just generally playing, have a toy potty nearby. Perhaps the toys are having a tea party and say "Oh, your doll thinks she has to go to the toilet. She can feel the wee down here [point to either your or your toddler's bladder area]. Quick, squeeze tight Dolly and jump up and run to the toilet."

Demonstrate with the doll as she stops playing, jumps up and says, "Oh, I can feel a wee coming, quick squeeze my muscles (or hold on) and run to the toilet room." Act this through.

As dolly gets to the toilet/potty, say "Quick Dolly, pull your pants down, hold on tight to the wee." Then sit the doll down on the toilet and say "Ah, that's it, now relax, relax those muscles and sit and wait for the wee to come out."

Wait.

Say "Here it comes; it comes out fast and pshhhhh!" Make the sound of wee coming out.

Once finished, say "Let's wait a little longer until it stops dripping." Now we need to wipe. Break a little toilet paper (it's a great idea to count squares – maybe 3-6) or get a little wet wipe. Demonstrate dolly wiping from front to back. Say "Dolly wipes to keep herself clean." Place the wipe into the potty/toilet. (I often use tissues when demonstrating in my clinic).

Dolly stands up and pulls up her knickers. She looks into the potty/toilet and says, "Well done Dolly for doing your wee in the potty." If you are using a toilet then act out pressing the button to flush! Say "We do our wee/poos in the potty or toilet just like mummy".

Say "Now let's wash our hands"

Bella with her doll practicing on the potty.

READ BOOKS

As mentioned earlier, read some books about toilet training or you can even make your own if you are creative with a camera, computer and printer. Take photos of your child, their potty/toilet, your wipes, bathroom etc and make a personalised book on toilet training. If you are creative and create your own, we'd love to see your book; you can email us at info@babysmiles.com.au

Where to start with your own book? Simply think about each of the steps you are teaching your child about toilet training. Start with your child playing as the first step is to stop and realise they have to go. Next, have your toddler walking down the hallway to the toilet. Then have a picture of them in the toilet room. Keep going right up to washing and drying hands. This will be a great teaching tool to reinforce what your child is learning.

Yes, including a photo of the poo and wee is also a good idea as that is what it's all about - if you wish to!

Children learn by reading especially with friends

STEP 3 TELL THEM WHAT YOU ARE EXPECTING

The night before you plan to start simply explain to your toddler in his words that tomorrow he will need to do his wee in his potty.

Explain that if he thinks he feels a wee coming he needs to say "Mummy potty" and you will both run to the potty. He will pull his pants down, sit on it and do his wee in the potty. Explain that every time he has done a wee he will get a sticker on his sticker chart.

Tell him that you will help him to learn and he will practise during the day a lot.

STEP 4 STARTING TO LEARN AND PRACTICE

Today's the day – last night you prepped your toddler by telling him that today you expect him to learn how to do his wees on his potty. Make sure you are excited when you chat about this to your toddler.

Make sure that before the day begins you are certain about exactly what you are going to be doing, step by step and how to teach your toddler. To make it easier for you, here is an outline on what you are going to do for the first two days and from there, just keep going. Re-read this section a few times to be clear.

On day one you will need all your attention to be on your toddler so be organised, have everything ready and plan to stay home for the next few days at least. Try to not have any interruptions at all.

TOILET TRAINING DAY 1

Plan to stay home for the next few days at least.

Take the phone off the hook.

If you have other children, this is the time to ask grandma or dad or a friend to look after them so that you can just pay attention to your toddler that you are toilet training. You will then be able to do what you need to without interruptions or running back and forth between other children.

Work out which room/area of your house you will mainly stay in for the first day. It is easier if this room has no carpets or rugs to make cleaning up easier. The lounge room, living room, verandah or play room is ideal. Roll up any rugs and simply put them away for the next week or so.

There will certainly be accidents, so prepare yourself mentally to stay calm and be patient and it will be easier to do the cleaning up. Try and stay in this room for the most of your day. Ideally try to choose a room that is close to the toilet so that he does not have to run so far to the toilet.

If the room that is the most practical is a fair way from the toilet, then it might be more practical (for the first day only) to take the potty to the room you are in (just to make it that bit easier) and from the second day onwards move the potty to the toilet as this is where you are training his brain to go to. Make sure all your equipment is organised: the spare clothes, training pants, etc. Be sure you have everything you need. A great place to store all this is in the bathroom as most bedrooms are often carpeted.

Bella starting to learn the steps

Take the phone off the hook and turn your mobile off. You really need to focus on your toddler today.

Next, you need to be excited and when you talk about it to your toddler. Be really excited! If he wants to leave the room, just give a gentle reminder that 'today we are potty training and staying here'. It is only one day and if you are organised you will have plenty to do for the day.

When he wakes up on this day, remind him excitedly that today is the day that you start toilet training. Then go about your day as you normally would do and after breakfast go to the room you have picked, take his nappy off and put his training pants on. Avoid putting shorts over the top of his training pants, just have a shirt and training pants; we want to make it as easy as possible to remove clothing.

Encourage your toddler to drink lots and lots of water as this will make him want to go to the toilet and the more practice he has this first day, the quicker he will learn what you are trying to teach.

Explain to him in his words that he now has to do his wee in his potty. Explain that if he thinks he feels a wee coming he needs to say "Mummy potty" and you will both run to the potty, he will pull his pants down, sit on it and do his wee in the potty. Explain that every time he has done a wee he will get a sticker on his sticker chart.

Do a practice run to the potty so he knows what to do. I suggest doing this three times. Make sure this is realistic and he needs to pull his pants down by hooking his thumbs inside the elastic of his pants and pushing them down all the way to his ankles. Praise him for each little step along the way.

Make sure that as he sits down on the potty that his bottom is against the back of the potty. Show him how to push his penis pointing downwards, or for girls how to slightly tilt or tip her hips by leaning forward a little. Tell him why. Then pretend to do a wee, make the sound of wee going into the potty, praise him, get him to wipe then stand up and pull his training pants back up again. Then get a pretend reward i.e. Sticker, prize, whatever you have decided.

Remember to do the practice run three times. On the third practice run ask him to actually see if he can do a wee. Have him sit for about 5 minutes on the potty waiting with his hands on his knees. After 5 minutes if he hasn't done a wee, ask him to get up and check the potty. If there is no wee, just say 'Oh, no wee, next time, we'll try again later'.

Wait 15 minutes and try again. If you are using the potty watch, set the musical alarm for a 15-minute reminder. Your toddler can press the musical button a number of times to listen while they wait on the potty.

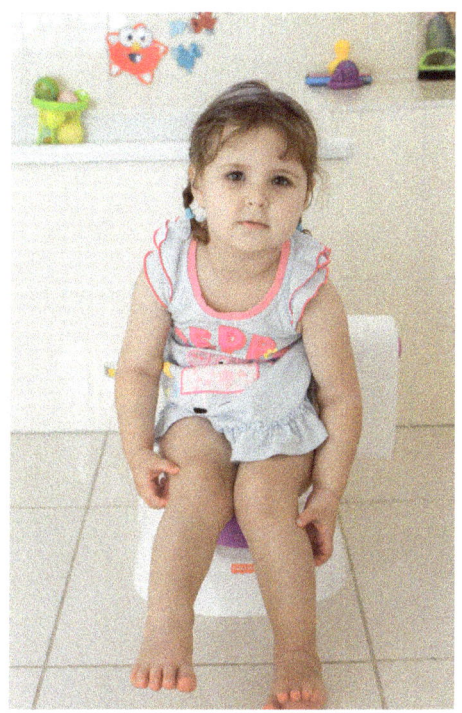

Isabella practicing on her potty

It may take about an hour of this at the start to actually get a wee in the potty and there may be a couple of accidents. Do not worry, this is okay. Just be positive and keep going. Don't get upset or show your toddler that you are upset.

When an accident happens (and it will) get him to run and sit on the potty anyway as we are also training his brain where to go. Get him to feel his pants and show him they are wet and the wet patch on the floor. Ask him to place his pants in the bucket

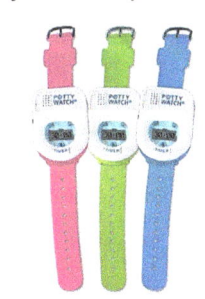

The Potty Time watch

which I'd have in the bathroom if the laundry is too far away. Follow through with him washing his hands. Remind him about the treat or the stickers if he does his wee in the potty. Then put a dry pair of pants on and talk about them being dry. Keep being positive and patient!

Use reward stickers for just trying

Then just go about your day playing and giving him drinks. Every ten minutes or so ask him if his pants are wet or dry? Get him to tell you. If they are dry, make a song and give him lots of praise. If they are already wet, get him to go to the potty and still try (as mentioned before) and change etc.

Now every 15 minutes you need to get him to sit on the potty for 5 minutes.

Eventually he will do a wee on the potty.

Make a big deal of this by singing, clapping, dancing and blowing party whistles that you can keep in the toilet just for this. When he has finished, show him how to tip the wee into the toilet and flush to wash the potty clean. Get him to wash his hands and then give him a sticker and/or treat. Make sure you emphasise how wonderful he is doing a wee and how happy you are, and how clever he is!

Praise: Make a big deal by singing, clapping, dancing and blowing party whistles, keep it positive.

Keep going all day, every 15 minutes. At rest time after lunch, be sure to explain that this is now the only time he will be using a nappy/pull-up during the day.

Once he wakes up from his daytime sleep, you need to take his nappy off and put him straight on the potty. This is an ideal time for him to wee. If he doesn't wee, that's okay.

Keep doing the same every 15 minutes for the afternoon. This will be a big day for you both, but be consistent and keep going. He will get the hang of weeing in the potty by the end of the day.

TOILET TRAINING DAY 2

On Day Two do exactly the same as Day One.

Once you notice that he is having lots of successes and fewer accidents and staying dry often (not always) then you don't have to have him sit on the potty so often; you can now stretch the 15 minutes to longer, say 30 minutes. If you are using the potty watch, simply change the timer to 30 minute reminders. I love the potty watch as it keeps children motivated and they love the musical reminders.

Once you notice that he is doing his wees in the potty one after the other you can also change what you say – so rather than telling him he must sit on the potty, instead ask – if he wants to go or needs to go?

Do the same as Day 1 in that if the wee is in the potty, you are very excited and happy, and if his pants are dry you are excited too. Give lots and lots of praise.

Don't worry too much about any accidents, just reinforce dry pants and wees in the potty and clean up as you did on Day 1.

By the end of Day 2 and Day 3 you will start to see a pattern in when your toddler needs to do a wee. They will also be able to hold on better than Day 1.

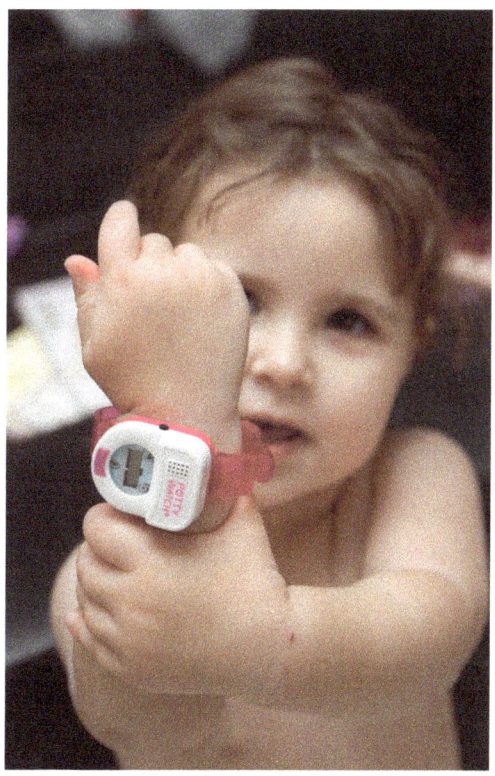

Bella enjoying her potty time watch

If you put the potty in the room you were playing in instead of the toilet, now would be the time to move it back to the toilet, so that it is always in the toilet and he doesn't have to worry where the potty could be. Explain to him and show him you are putting the potty into the toilet room and do a couple of practice runs so that his brain now knows where the potty is. You may also need to remind him when he tells you that 'quick run to the toilet' as the potty has moved from the previous day. Once again patience is the key.

Sitting to practise before and after a bath is an ideal time: Lilly after a bath trying on the potty

LEARN TO READ YOUR TODDLER'S BODY LANGUAGE

Your toddler certainly gives you signals that a wee or poo is on its way. If you can learn to read their body language, this will help you get him to the toilet on time. So here is a list of what to look for in body language...

WEE COMING

- Wriggling around, bouncing, squirming or what I call the 'potty dance'
- Rocking back and forth
- Holding their nappy area at the front
- Crossing their legs
- Moving from foot to foot, back and forth
- Squeezing their legs together
- Stopping what they are doing and holding still, like on pause
- Making a little noise
- Watch these times and be ready: first up in the morning upon waking, or after day sleep, about 20 – 45 minutes after drinking, before a bath or as you run the bath water

POO COMING

- Making 'wind'
- Squatting down

- Touching their nappy underneath
- Grunting or pushing noises
- Bending
- Stopping what they are doing and bending their knees
- Watch these times and be ready: 20 minutes after breakfast or after/during running around post meal,

Adapted Pantley 2007

WIPING

Wiping your bottom until it is clean is something we as adults don't spend too much time thinking about, let alone discussing. For your child this skill is just one part of toilet training that they need to learn. It's a tricky one! It takes lots of practice and most likely will still need lots of practice after holding on and getting to the toilet is mastered.

First of all, like any new skill you need to show your child what to do, get them to practice and then help them to make sure it is done completely. Again, you can also practice on their doll as well.

The steps involved are:

- Getting the right amount of paper – not too much and not too little – perhaps counting the squares before you rip it off will help
- Too little and it gets messy; too much and it's hard to manage

- Wiping from front to back – especially with girls because you don't want to wipe the poo towards their vagina as this can cause urinary infection issues at times

- Wiping and looking at the paper until it is clean

- Learning when to get some more fresh paper

- With particularly sticky bottoms, I recommend having some flushable wet wipes in the toilet that can be used to help clear the 'sticky bottom'. After use, they should be placed in the toilet and flushed away with the paper.

- If your child has 'skid' marks on their undies then they also need to know how to deal with these. Have a system. For example, place dirty undies in the laundry basket or in the laundry sink or a specific bucket. Get them to do this and let you know if need be.

- Remember your language, use of words; be sure not to talk about stinky, yucky poos while cleaning or with accidents, just keep it matter of fact. Poos are simply a bodily function.

Nicole's Tip:

How to measure how much toilet paper to use? Try counting the squares (say 4-6) or measure an arm's stretch length or roll it until it just touches the floor.

Is your toddler rolling out way too much toilet paper? Then try this trick: simply squeeze the roll a little, so that it flattens out, this doesn't stop it unravelling but slows down the amount that your toddler pulls out. So instead of a circular-round roll it should look more oval-egg shaped once you have given it a squeeze.

Getting the right amount of paper can be tricky – not too much and not too little – try counting the squares before they rip it off will help

HAND WASHING

Hand washing often seems to be optional when going to the toilet but it shouldn't be.

Hand washing is one simple step that is the most important in stopping the spread of germs and disease. So it's really important to teach your toddler right from the beginning of toilet training that hand washing is just one step in the whole process.

Hand washing: a simple but important step

So after each trip to the toilet, whether they have 'done something or not' as soon as they finish in the toilet room they need to go to the bathroom and wash their hands with soap.

Hopefully before you start toilet training this is a skill that they have already been practising so just add it into their routine. It's not a skill that is easily mastered after one lesson, so be prepared to show them again and again how to wash their hands correctly with soap.

They must learn to squeeze the soap, rub it on their palms, the back of their hands and up and down each finger – a good plan is to get them to rub all these parts of their hands at least twice, so that any that is missed the first time hopefully gets a soaping the second time. They then need to learn how to wash off the soap properly and then wipe dry on a towel. If you use a hand towel be sure to explain this to your toddler too.

Handwashing after flushing is very important

Nicole's Tip:

Make sure the soap is child friendly, that they can pump-squirt the bottle easily or reach the soap. I also love the Aqueduck water spout extender: a simple, silicon design that fits onto your spout to redirect the water closer to the edge of the bathroom sink to make it so much easier for your toddler to reach the water (designed by a parent of course!) and it saves your back from lifting them. These really work!

The Aqueduck water spout extender is brilliant for little children

Aqueduck come in 4 great colours.

Have a look in our online shop for more toilet training tips, articles and charts www.babysmiles.com.au

STEP 5 PRAISE AND ENCOURAGEMENT

Praise and encouragement are a big part of teaching your toddler about toilet training. There are many different ways you can encourage them.

The best method of all, which I've spoken about previously, is your praise and attention. Pay attention to what you want – which is dry pants, doing wees and poos into the potty or toilet, and/or them telling you they need to go. You will always have your praise and attention with you no matter where you are. You may not have the star chart or the prize box. Anyway, you are mum and dad. Your toddler loves you and loves your attention.

You cannot spoil your toddler with words of encouragement and lots of high five's, kisses and praise when they are trying, co-operating and being successful. This should be their biggest reward.

YOU CAN PRAISE YOUR TODDLER BY:

- Smiling
- Clapping
- Dancing
- High-fiving
- Talking about how successful they were at telling you, getting there, doing a wee, pulling their pants down, washing their hands; in fact, every little step
- Touching and cuddles
- Singing
- Making eye contact
- Playing

If you are patient, kind, encouraging and excited when helping them to learn, they in turn will learn quickly and confidently.

Bella enjoying her mum's love and attention

You will always have your praise and attention with you no matter where you are. Your toddler loves you and your attention.

There are also other ways we keep children motivated and focused and here are a few other ideas to help and to show progress:

STAR CHART

Children love star charts – so use the chart provided at the back of this book, or join our member section on our website www.babysmiles.com.au and simply print one out every time you need it. At the beginning place a sticker, tick or stamp on the chart every time your child 'tries' – that is, sits on the potty and practises. You are aiming for about every 15 minutes to 30 minutes the first few days.

A potty watch is also a great reminder for children that it's time to go and sit and practice. Parents can set the alarm for a time and when the alarm goes (which may involve music and/or flashing lights) it's time to go to the toilet room and sit on the potty and practice.

Star charts are a wonderful way to keep a track of when you child has successes – so when there is a poo or a wee (it doesn't matter how much) in the potty put a different coloured sticker on or stamp. You may also consider using a reward or prize box for actual success to keep the motivation going, though this is not necessary.

Nicole's Tip:

Encourage your child to place the sticker/stamp on the chart. This helps keep them motivated and it's not just the parent that wants to learn this new skill.

Keep your star charts and look back over them to see progress.

REWARDS

Having a prize box is an idea I love. All children love to get a little prize as a reward for reaching a goal. The trick here is one to make the prize 'little'. I suggest going to the $2 shop or a party supply place and finding little packs of prizes. Some ideas are little toy plastic animals, bouncy balls, stick on earrings, tiny bubble-blowing bottles, mini play-doh, fat crayons, anything small – just open the packets and tip the prizes into a colourful cardboard present box.

Nicole's prize box with stickers, balls, pencils, rubbers, mini playdoh

Be clear about when and for what your child receives a reward. They can pick and choose from the box.

My suggestion would be at the end of the first day – where there are a number of stickers on the chart just for 'trying' – they can choose from the prize box. After 2 or 3 days of this, change the goal to after doing a poo (or part of one) or a wee on the potty/toilet. They get to choose each time.

Once again, after 3 or 4 or 5 days of a reward in a row, change the goal again. For example, after a successful day of all poos being deposited in the potty, they can choose a reward.

The overall aim is for parents to keep children motivated, which can be fulfilled by making sure you have set achievable goals. At first, it will be relatively easy for your child to be able to choose a reward and get stickers. However, after a short time, make it just a little harder.

Stretch out the reward (say, for staying dry) to lunchtime or to the end of the whole day, which then becomes stretched again after two days in a row etc.

The motivation from rewards and sticker charts will naturally fade away once your child is in the habit of doing the steps of toilet training. Then they start to forget to put the stickers on and quickly catch up, and then they forget again and quite naturally they move past the charts and rewards as using the potty is now just part of the everyday routine.

The motivation from sticker charts will naturally fade away.

 Nicole's Tip:

I'm not a big fan of rewarding children with lollies or chocolates for sitting and trying to do something in the potty. There are other types of rewards that work equally well. One mum I knew, who was inspired by my balloon reward box (just a shiny box filled with colourful balloons), used just balloons as a reward every time there was a success on the potty as that was what her child loved.

So if your child has a love of an item (whether it be hairclips or animals), there is certainly motivation for collecting the whole set in the prize box! Make sure you open the packet and put individual items in the prize box, so that each one is a separate reward. Do not give them the whole packet!

TRY THE LUCKY DIP TREASURE BOWL

As an alternative to the Prize Box where children get to choose their own prize, here is another version, which parents find just as popular and successful.

Again, go to the shop and get about 30 little inexpensive prizes. Make sure they are only little. Wrap each prize separately or if it's a pack of animals/hairclips etcetera, break it up into individual prizes and wrap them in nice colourful paper. Place them all in a clear plastic bowl on the bathroom bench; this is your Lucky Dip Treasure Bowl. Tell your toddler that these are 'Potty Prizes'. Each time they are successful at doing a wee or a poo in the potty they can choose a prize. Tell them to let you know when they are ready to start. Most toddlers will be ready right now! Some though will look at the bowl for a day or two and then announce they are ready.

You can use this with the sticker chart so you can map progress (be sure to only talk about the successes). Each time your toddler goes to the potty and it is successful, they get to choose a prize. Gradually the bowl starts to empty. By the time the bowl is empty your toddler should well and truly be on their way to being toilet trained. (Elizabeth Pantley 2007)

If your toddler requests more prizes when the bowl is empty, simply do a room search together and rewrap some of the previous prizes. It doesn't worry them that it's the same prize rewrapped – they know – it's the unwrapping that excites a toddler. They will love this just as much as a new prize, believe me! At some stage they will move past the prizes and unwrapping and forget about the prizes altogether if you continue to praise and take notice of all the successes in the potty.

STEP 6 PROMPTS

After the first few days of telling your toddler to go to the toilet at regular timed intervals, you then need to start moving to 'prompting' your toddler instead.

Once you notice that he is doing his wees in the potty one after the other you need to change what you say – so rather than telling him he must sit on the potty, instead ask: "Do you need to or want to go to the toilet?"

ACCIDENTS

Without a doubt there will be numerous times when accidents happen, so expect them. This is all part of the learning process. No one ever learns a new skill and gets it right 100% of the time! Your attitude here is essential. Despite the frustration, busyness and annoyance of 'yet again', you must respond to accidents very matter-of-factly.

Say something like 'It's okay, let's just get to the potty." Continue to take your child to the potty despite the puddle on the floor.

Why? Because you are training their brain where to go. Straight to the toilet. Success or not. You still need to run, walk, go to the toilet. Go through the entire process of sitting them on their potty even though you know it has all come out. It is about training their brain. Get them to wait patiently for a few minutes or longer. Then proceed with the normal process of wiping, cleaning up, changing pants, washing hands. When this is all done, go back and clean up the accident without further comment. This includes sighing, rolling eyes, stomping, or comments of exasperation. Any criticism can demotivate your child and make them hesitate to tell you about accidents in case they get into trouble.

Children should never be in trouble for accidents. Accidents can happen when

- Your child is very tired
- Your child is sick
- Too busy playing
- Too excited
- Upset
- Cold
- Too much sugary foods

TIPS FOR BOYS

Sitting or standing? This is a question that only parents of boys need to consider. Undoubtedly, my advice is 'sitting'.

Why? Firstly, toddlers usually find it easier to toilet train with their poos first and the wees soon follow (it can be the other way around too). Often a poo unexpectedly comes out while they are sitting on the toilet waiting for the wee, and it is a bit of a surprise. If your son is standing, this is unlikely to happen. Then you have to teach a whole other idea of sitting for poos rather than one following the other quite naturally. So then you are teaching two separate jobs: wees and then poos rather than the two together.

For a poo to come out, toddlers must be able to sit and learn to relax their muscles and wait for the poo. Often there is pushing involved – unlike wee – so that once toddlers learn to relax their muscles, the poo can shoot out quite quickly. So teaching your son to sit and wait and relax will work for both wees and poos.

Another great reason for teaching boys to sit is aim. It is much easier to teach a boy to just push his penis into the toilet a little or behind the plastic guard on the front of the toilet seat or potty so that the wee shoots down when he is able to relax and let go. It is much harder to teach aim.

Usually it is around the age of 3 or 4 years that a boy is naturally interested in learning to stand to do a wee and then, of course, aim should be taught. There are lots of little fun tricks that are not necessary but certainly make learning to aim a game. Like toilet targets, toilet floatable 'food' or 'toys' to hit. Your son also needs to be tall enough to be able to stand and aim into the bowl. There are also toilet products which have little cups especially designed for boys that hang on the side of the toilet; however these can be messy to tip and rinse and clean.

My best advice, keep boys on a potty or toilet sitting for as long as possible. Teach him to hold his penis down towards the bowl so the stream of wee goes downwards.

DO'S & DON'TS OF TOILET TRAINING

Do make sure your child is ready	Don't start because you are ready and want to save money
Do praise all trying, successes and telling you after the fact	Don't punish for accidents and telling you too late
Do use easy to remove clothing	Don't use overalls, tricky clips, buttons and zip clothing
Do give your child healthy, sugar free food, lots of fruit and vegetables and yoghurt to help with loose poos	Don't give sugary foods and drinks as this makes the bladder itchy or lots of carbohydrates as this can cause constipation

Do give lots of extra water to drink to help stretch the bladder	Don't avoid giving water drinks thinking it will help
Do be patient and calm	Don't sigh, roll your eyes, scold or yell when you are tired
Do make sure your toddler gets enough sleep	Don't keep your toddler up late then expect them to learn a new skill
Do be consistent and keep to a routine	Don't chop and change between training and not training
Do make sure you are organised and know where the toilet is when you are out	Don't have no idea where the nearest toilet is

Common Questions – Expert Answers

Of course Toilet Training doesn't always go smoothly, so included here are the most common questions parents ask and all my expert answers.

ASKING TOO LATE

All children start off the toilet training process by telling you AFTER they have done a wee or poo in their pants. Be patient. This is actually a good sign that one, they are noticing and stopping what they are doing, and two, feeling confident enough to come and tell you that it has already happened.

Praise her for coming and telling you and taking notice and then just deal with it matter-of-factly. Still go to the toilet and if it is a poo try as best you can to tip it into the toilet. Go through the clean up in the toilet just as you would normally do. It's even a good idea to still get your toddler to sit on the potty/toilet for a few minutes as you normally would. We are training their brain where to go and where the wee and poos are to go.

Whatever you do, don't get cranky or annoyed with them or make negative comments. This will only make them afraid to tell you and toilet training will definitely go backwards.

Just clean up and move on. If it is happening a lot then definitely use the sticker sheet for 'successful' wees and poos so they can visually see their successes.

CONSTIPATION

We all get a little constipated at times but it is most important to make sure your toddler ISN'T constipated during the toilet training process and in the months following.

Why? Learning to push a poo out takes a bit more effort than a wee and if that poo is hard, lumpy or really big, it hurts! Once it hurts, your child in their brain will go: "Hmmm that hurts, when I am doing a poo on the potty. How can I stop or avoid this in future? Oh, don't do poos! Just hold onto them. That's a good idea."

Now you see! Unlike us adults, they do not quite understand the link between diet and poos. Good healthy foods with lots and lots of water means soft, sausage- like poos. So really make sure that their diet is centered on healthy foods: fruit and veggies, yoghurts and lots of water. Avoid juices, sugary drinks/food, and carbohydrates.

Look at their poos and aim for the long smooth sausage (see the Bristol Stool Chart in this book). If their poos show signs of cracks, hardness or little balls breaking off, then make some dietary changes immediately. Give your toddler lots more water or watery fruits and veggies – cut down on the pasta, bread, potatoes etc. We really want to avoid the 'holding onto the poo' mindset.

The Bristol Stool Chart is at the back of this book*

DAYCARE & BABYSITTERS

Most daycare centres are very experienced in toilet training and are usually telling parents that their child is ready to start toilet training. So if your centre brings this up with you then seriously consider their advice, no matter how busy you are. They will only be telling you this and bringing it to your attention because your child is really ready to start and showing all the signs needed to begin.

Often at daycare, children do developmental steps earlier because there are lots of other children to watch and copy unlike at home where there may only be an older or younger sibling if any.

Once you have decided to start and you have read through the checklist and know your child is ready, then be sure to have a conversation with the daycare staff, your nanny or any sitters that you will be using and let them know the plan and what you are doing. If your child is at daycare often, then this plan should really be developed together with the staff so that both parents and staff are doing the same steps and the same type of reminders and have the same expectations. This will be better for your child and less confusing.

Once you start or the staff at daycare start, you need to be consistent and do the same at home no matter how tempting it is to 'just put the nappy back on and have a backup plan' because you are busy. Toilet training will be quicker if you are consistent and less confusing for your toddler. Be consistent and it won't take long. And your toddler will be saying 'goodbye' to nappies during the day.

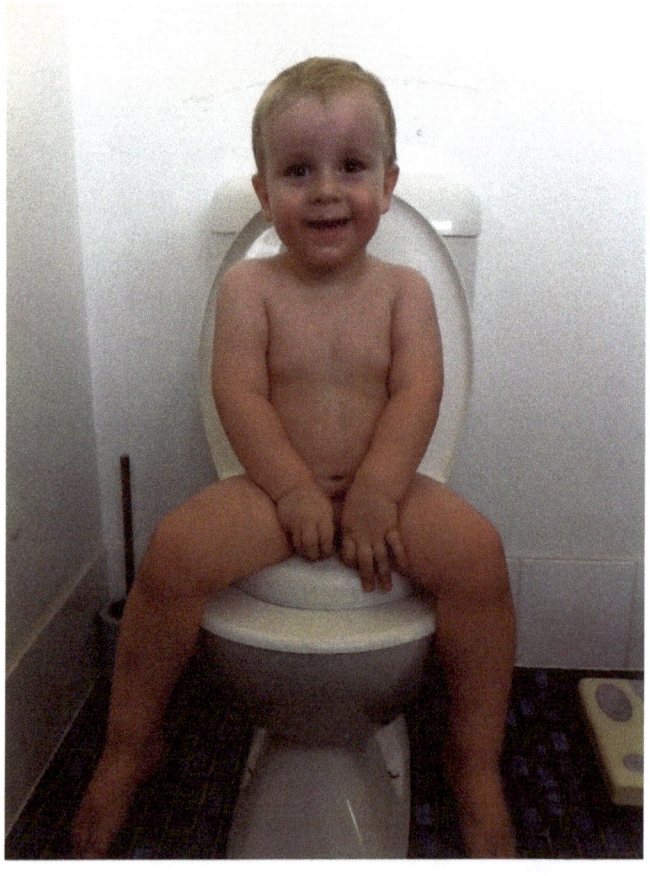

Soon you will be saying goodbye to Nappies

If you are running into difficulties with daycare staff and they are reluctant to start training and you believe it may be because they are very busy, then again consider keeping your child at home for the week and starting on a Saturday. In my experience most centres are very keen to help parents start their child in the new skill and are very supportive of your efforts.

DON'T FLUSH IT, IT'S MINE!

Okay this certainly happens. Why? Some children see their poo as part of themselves. Often a clue is when they say and wave goodbye to it before they flush it down the toilet. Don't worry, this is normal and is fine. However it is better if you don't initiate this or help them to do so. This is making the poo too personal. We want them just to see it as waste product that comes out, not part of themselves.

FEAR

As a follow on to the above 'constipation', fear occurs once your toddler has had a difficult, hard poo that hurt very much. They might logically think they will hold on but the basis of this 'holding on' is fear. They become scared of the poo hurting them. And once again their brain makes illogical links like 'it is okay to do a poo in your nappy but not the toilet,' because they remember doing it in their nappy and it didn't hurt. Or they think that 'It is okay to do a poo in your undies but not the potty.' Again they remember doing it in their undies and all was fine.

All the problems like holding on, nappy only, undies only and bedroom but not toilet room are fear based. The only way forward then is to talk about their fears, challenge them step by step and test if their logical thoughts are actually right in a very patient way. If you need help to do this, please see a professional psychologist who can help with these issues.

GOING BACKWARDS – REGRESSION

Toddlers and older children can regress with toilet training. Regression is when they were day trained and had dry pants for a number of months or years then start to go backwards with wet pants at least twice a day, every day.

First of all, focus on the dry pants and get them to tell you when they need to go and just pay a little extra attention to what you want. Do not make a big deal of the wet pants. At the same time make sure that your child is well and you may like to rule out urinary tract infection or sickness.

The common reasons children regress are because

- They are just losing interest in toilet training
- They are looking for attention
- There has been a change in family life
- They don't have enough sleep

Some children lose interest because after a few weeks they decide that stopping what they are doing and going to the toilet is really just a hassle. They'd rather keep playing! To solve this problem you need to make it worthwhile for them to stop what they are doing, press pause on the play, get up and go to the toilet or the potty. Your toddler would have had a lot of attention at the beginning of toilet training so you need to go back a few steps and do all the cheering, clapping and whistle blowing that happened at the beginning again. Make it worthwhile for your child.

Sometimes this doesn't solve the problem as your child has decided just to let it go while they are busy and wet their pants. They have worked out that when they do come (at a time convenient for them) and tell you, you will drop everything, quickly change their pants for them so they will be nice and dry and then they can go back to their game or puzzle. Remember, this is all at their convenience so you need not be so quick to jump and help them.

Regression – go back to lots of praise and encouragement as you did at the beginning – make a big deal

My advice is to make them wait. Have an absorbent mat or spot for them to sit and wait and say something like "I just need to finish getting the lunch ready, you will need to sit on the towel and wait for me." Make her wait for 5 minutes because she needs to experience the consequence of being wet and how uncomfortable it is (without getting into trouble). She will then not be very happy as she is missing out on going back to her play. In a few minutes, simply say, "Mummy is ready now, let's go and get changed." Change her as you would normally. At this point, get her to put her wet pants into the bucket in the laundry or whatever your system is for dealing with wet pants. Again, let her experience the natural consequences, no rousing though! Just be patient.

While you are changing her, be sure to talk about how much quicker it would have been if she used the potty and she would be back to her puzzle earlier. Just point it out. She will work it out herself quickly!

I recommend the same strategy for children who are looking for attention; you will know if your child is one of these as he will come and find you and announce very proudly that he 'has wet his pants'. Praise dry pants and any other times he tells you he needs to go and use the 5 minute rule for natural consequences.

If you feel your child is regressing due to a change in your family the advice is somewhat different. Change in families covers a new baby, death of a grandparent, moving house, illness of a family member, moving cities, shared care or any other major change. Your toddler is reacting to the change and stress that is a result. Your instinct is probably to give them some lee-way and not force the issue and to just go backwards a little and start using pull-ups again.

My advice would actually be the opposite. Your toddler is saying, "I'm upset, I don't feel safe." As psychologists, we know that children, toddlers included, feel more emotionally secure and safe when the rules stay the same and the boundaries are drawn. So my advice is to keep going with your expectations of toilet training and be firm about them.

If you go backwards in this situation, you are reinforcing to your toddler that 'change is no good, it is scary and you are not safe.' Of course we want to give them the opposite feeling so keep the rules, keep your expectations and your toddler will feel secure and safe again. Say clearly that they still need to do their wee on the potty.

Re-read this book and go back to your rewards and give attention for using the potty and dry pants. Do not take too much notice of wet pants, accidents or telling you too late, just be matter-of-fact when dealing with this.

The exception to this is if there has been quite a lot of trauma and you are feeling that you cannot cope with the toilet training. Then ask yourself this: can another family member help you out to do this? Or perhaps a friend? If so, keep going. If not, then it's fine to take a break and stop toilet training for now. The same applies if you have shared care and the other parent is not taking the same interest or has the same goals for achieving dryness.

Simply take a break.

GOING OUTSIDE

Children are often outside and the temptation to let them go outside in a garden bed is great, especially when toilet training.

Just a word of warning with this one: be careful because I have certainly seen some very frustrated parents when their toddler refuses to use toilets as they enjoy going outside because it is more convenient. As an emergency, go outside for sure! All parents have been on the side of the road with a toddler who gives them 30 seconds of notice. In rural areas this is easier to deal with than in cities. I suggest you carry a portable potty just for this purpose, more so if you have a daughter. These are rather affordable.

Some toddlers are able to know the difference between going outside in their backyard and in the garden bed at kindy with ease yet for others it can be difficult to understand the idea that in one place it's allowed and another it's certainly not! So if your toddler is struggling with this, then for a while anyway you may need to have a 'toilet only' policy for wees and poos.

If they persist in doing poos outside in the garden, then they need to pick them up with a flushable wipe or toilet paper and put them where they belong in the toilet.

HE HAS TANTRUMS WHENEVER I ASK HIM TO SIT AND TRY

Often I have parents that ask me or email me about their toddler who isn't co-operating with toilet training. You thought they were ready and you were ready, but perhaps they co-operated for a day to two or a week then simply refused to try.

If they are having a tantrum about even sitting and trying then it's likely that it is too much stress, too much pressure or it seen as a punishment by your toddler.

Either way you have two options. First if it going badly and you are frustrated and annoyed and they are having tantrums at the very mention of everything potty or toilet related then you may need to just stop training. Have a break. Wait 6-8 weeks then try again, and start off very positively by taking note of their successes and not talking, sighing or mentioning the not so good tries.

The second option is to make it fun, so if you are hesitant to stop and you were off to a good start but somewhere along the way it became stressful (perhaps you were rushing the process or frustrated at the accidents) it's more than likely that it's not fun anymore for your toddler. Thus their tantrums are their way of telling you, "I don't want to, I don't like this pressure."

Re-read this book and make sure you add in the reading of books, the singing of songs and chatting to your toddler as they sit and wait. Stay home for the week and don't try to do toilet training away from home and go back to making a game of it. Toilet training away from home is naturally more stressful for mums as you wonder if they will make into the toilet in time in the shopping centre

You should notice a change in your toddler's attitude at once when you become less stressed and more playful about the whole learning experience. Perhaps also adjust your expectations, your toddler will have accidents and will not produce a wee or a poo every time they sit.

So if they don't produce anything when they sit, this is practising and training their brain where to go so it is not a waste of time. Make it fun again; you will soon see your toddler respond. Take your toddler regularly again. Give him a prize; add a sticker, clap, sing and phone Grandma to tell the good news! His motivation will come back.

I NEED YOU

Some children just love to have company while they are sitting on the potty. At the beginning you definitely need to stay with your toddler while they are learning. If you are there reading books or singing songs while they relax, sit and wait until something happens, they will sit and stay. Without a parent, often they will give it a 30 second go, announce loudly that nothing is happening or they don't need to go even though they just haven't waited long enough for their body to relax and then let go.

After they become more independent with toilet training, they should be happy to amuse themselves, sit there, read a book or sing some songs or nursery rhymes by themselves. Some children though, start to panic at the thought of mummy or daddy popping out to the kitchen or laundry and coming back in a few minutes. This becomes a problem quite quickly. And their reaction is more like a fear where they literally panic at the thought of you moving away. If this is happening then you need to break it into steps and gradually withdraw yourself bit by bit. So make a plan and it will look something like the following, though if you need more professional help to do this then seek advice.

- Stay in the toilet with your toddler
- Stand half in and half out of the door. If your child copes with this, then gradually extend how far you stand or sit.
- Stand in the hallway
- Walk away for 1 sec then come back into view, talking as you go
- Walk away for 5 sec then come back into view, talking on and off
- Walk away and don't talk
- Gradually extend the amount of time that you come and go, making it longer all the time

This is likely to take a couple of weeks to do.

I WILL MAKE YOU

If you are falling into the trap of 'trying to make' your child sit on the potty or co-operate then you are fighting a losing battle. You child is most likely to win as they have more energy, time and determination than parents. So if you are 'making them' then you are playing the wrong game. It becomes like a game of tug-o-war.

My advice is to sidestep the game and not tug back. Just give it a rest, wait and go back to the initial strategies of getting ready: your toddler watching you, role-playing with toys etc. in a casual way. Try again in another month or two.

IN THE CAR

Once you start to toilet train, one of the biggest worries for parents when going out is – what if they have to go when we are in the car? What if they wet the car seat?

At this stage, you can consider a few options. One is to leave your toddler in their training pants, jocks or knickers and put a pull-up nappy over the top so they still get the feeling of wetness if they do a wee before you can stop and get out of the car.

Another is to put a toilet training mat down on the car seat; these are disposable and act like a lining to protect the fabric.

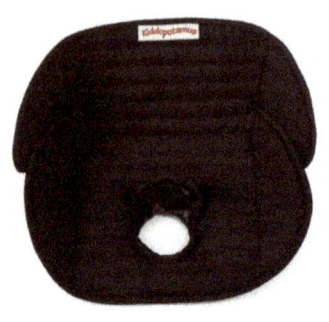 

Then be ready to stop at a moment's notice. Saying to a toddler to hold on in the first weeks of toilet training is unrealistic, so as soon as they say they have to go to the toilet you have about 30 seconds to stop the car safely and get them out on the side of the road and help them go to the toilet. The types of clothes you choose to dress them in will be enormously important – this is where teaching girls and wearing dresses is a bonus. For boys, make sure they can take their shoes and pants off quickly. Again, a great option here is the portable potty.

I'VE TRIED EVERYTHING...

Often a parent will say to me, that they have 'tried everything and nothing is working.' Sometimes the problem may be just that you have tried lots of different strategies trying to find the one that works and it is just too inconsistent for your toddler. Other times it is simply that your toddler is not ready even if you are and you have started too early. If either of these are true, then it's time to take a break for about six weeks, re-read this book, get organised then start again.

Car travel: on the side of the road with Miley and her portable potty

Occasionally I see toddlers who actually get lots of attention for 'not' co-operating with toilet training. They might get lots of payoffs for having 'accidents', i.e. they get more attention, talking to, one on one time with mummy, conversations, explanations and just plain reactions (even cranky ones) and the whole process has become a game. If this is your situation, then be sure to payoff what you want: dry pants, saying they need to go, using the potty. Do not pay any attention to the wet pants, accidents etc. Your toddler should change their attitude in two or three days.

If this isn't successful then just stop, take no more notice of toilet training, stop talking about it, put away the sticker charts, the prize boxes and just simply go back to nappies and be matter-of-fact about it. Don't play the game. Sidestep it altogether.

At some point, your toddler is likely to ask about it. That's fine, discuss it if they bring it up, but focus purely on success – dry pull-ups, telling you they need to do a poo, washing hands co-operatively, and stop all attention if they are being difficult or not co-operating. Wait. Do not do battle over toilet training.

Then again in a month or two, when they are more co-operative, set the scene. Bring out the sticker charts, the rewards and the prizes. Talk about it and try again.

If your toddler is overtired then they will definitely be way less co-operative and tend to do battle over every little thing. Fix their sleep first before attempting toilet training.

MOVING FROM POTTY TO TOILET

At some point, once your toddler is comfortable using the potty on the floor, they will be ready to progress to the big toilet. When? The sooner the better for parents as it's convenient to be able to use a toilet anywhere. However, be led by your child in this process. Some children are curious and comfortable with trying new things, toilets included, whereas others like to just stay with what is comfortable and familiar and may panic when using the big toilet.

Oops sometimes backwards works too

Either way, wait until your toddler shows an interest and asks about using the big toilet. Be sure you are ready to start before you put them on the toilet. This means having a stepping stool that is really, really stable or stairs for them to climb up. Nothing makes a child regress more than getting a fright climbing up to the big toilet or slipping and somewhat falling in. So if you are at home then you need to use the child toilet seat insert that fits snuggly over the adult toilet seat so there is no risk of them falling in. If you are out, either carry the portable folding child insert, usually in a little carry bag or you will need to hold them for the whole time that they are on the toilet.

When not to do it? Don't let them use the big toilet if they are afraid of it. The size might be daunting, or it might be the noise of flushing. Don't push it, leave it.

They will be ready at some stage.

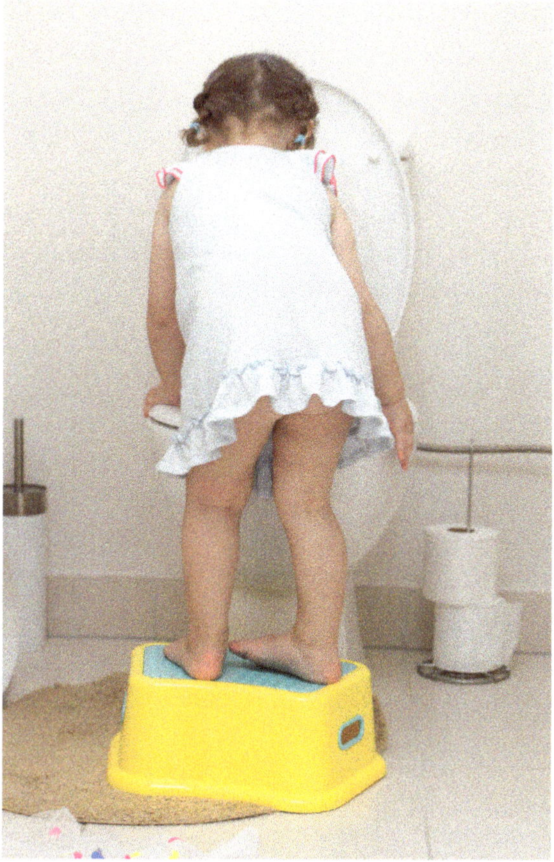

 Nicole's Tip:

Still keep the potty around for any emergencies. For example, when you may not be able to come straight away and they are taking themselves to the toilet they may be in a hurry and do not have time to climb up, or when they get up during the night.

Set the scene by talking about the big toilet for a few days beforehand. Talk about how it is different to the potty, why adults use it and show them other types of toilets when out n about. Then just practise sitting on the big toilet. It is quite okay to practise with clothes on if that is what they prefer just to see how it feels rather than have expectations of it being successful. If they are in a hurry, avoid using the big toilet as you don't want a negative experience. Before you know it, your toddler will be choosing the big toilet more and more.

- Make sure your toddler is really ready
- Talk about the big toilet
- Get a stable step stool or stairs
- Use a child adapter toilet seat
- Just try with clothes on
- Let them choose

MY POTTY AND ONLY MINE!

Some toddlers become quite confident with their own potty and are very, very reluctant to use another potty or toilet. Whether they are just more cautious, more sensitive or more possessive, they often want to take their potty with them and will panic or refuse to use another potty or toilet. That's quite okay – just go with it.

Bella transitioning from potty to toilet

Take your potty with you or buy a second one that sits in the car. This refusal to use another potty can also be the same for the child-sized toilet seats that fit over the adult toilet. Again, just go with it. Buy a second toilet seat, put it into a plastic bag and have it in the boot of your car or under the pram in the basket for when you need it. This situation will pass in time as they become more confident and more flexible. A foldable portable seat in a bag is a great idea!

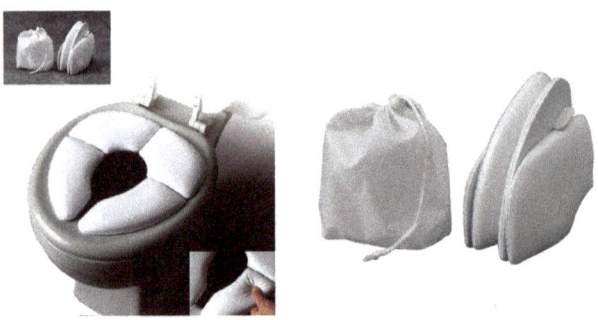

If your toddler is using the big toilet, when you are out and about this portable seat is ideal. It is soft, folds into four pieces and comes with a travel bag, great for the back of the car or the bottom of your pram.

NIGHT CONTROL

When does your toddler start being dry at night? Once you have achieved daytime dryness, this is a really important question. My best answer to this is that generally it is a good twelve months after daytime dryness is happening (it can certainly be years later). Night-time dryness has nothing to do with toilet training – it is a very separate topic and will only happen if your child's body is developmentally ready.

Of course, like everything related to children and development, there are certainly children who are interested and can be dry all night after six months from achieving daytime dryness or it may take until six years of age. There is a vast difference in age from daytime dryness to night-time dryness. A word of warning here is that night-time dryness will never be achieved, no matter how much mum or dad wish for it, until your child's body developmentally can do this.

There is more involved in night time dryness than daytime and it is often a much harder skill. It is considered normal if there is still night-time wetness until the age of six years.

Just keep using nappies or pull-ups at night-time and for daytime sleeps. As soon as your toddler wakes from their daytime sleep, encourage them to sit on the potty straight away – the same for waking first up in the morning after sleeping all night.

As soon as you notice that their nappy during the daytime sleep is dry about three days in a row, take it off for daytime sleeps only. Continue to use a nappy at night-time, as holding for two hours is very different to holding for twelve hours all night. Talk to your toddler about holding onto their wee in their bladder while they sleep, then when their bladder is too full, their brain needs to wake their body up and tell them to get up and go to the toilet and empty their bladder.

Now the rule is the same for night-time. Once you have noticed dry nappies upon waking for three, four or five nights in a row, immediately start night time training. If you wait and delay, then after a week or two your toddler (more likely than not) will lose motivation, shrug their shoulders and say, "Oh well, I have a nappy on so I can just let it go," and you will miss the window of opportunity.

I can't stress this enough: night-time dryness is a different process to daytime training. Apart from not being biologically ready – i.e. their bladder isn't yet stretchy enough to hold twelve hours' worth of urine, their brain isn't listening to the signals while they are asleep or they may overproduce urine at night – the other main reason some children take a lot longer to be dry at night than other children is hereditary. Diabetes, food sensitivities (especially dairy, fruit and chocolate), medication and other health problems can also be reasons for night-time bladder control issues. As your child grows, their body should self correct these issues, so don't stress just go with it for the moment.

Waterproof mattress protector to keep the mattress dry

Once you decide to remove the night-time nappy, it's a great idea to put a waterproof mattress protector underneath your cloth sheet if you haven't already done so.

Nicole's Tip:

An awesome tip here to save you time during the night is to have two or even three layers already made up: a waterproof protector, cotton sheet, waterproof protector, cotton sheet etc. So if you need to change the sheets during the night, simply strip off the top sheet and protector and your toddler's bed is ready to go. If there are any night-time accidents, remember to reassure your toddler that all children have this happen. Praise a dry bed the next morning and be sure to put your toddler straight onto the potty when they wake in the morning.

PROFESSIONAL HELP

If you have questions or concerns about any aspect of toilet training or you are dealing with a toddler who is fearful, holding onto wee or poo or being really defiant, rather than wait and hope that your child will grow out of it, sometimes all that is needed is one consultation with a professional who works in this area to give you a plan of action, or answer your questions and concerns with expert advice. So contact your doctor, psychologist or contact our clinic on info@babysmiles.com.au for more information. We do online parenting help via skype, facetime, phone or email packages and will be able to assist you.

PUNISHMENT

All parents get tired, frustrated, annoyed and angry at times. This is usually to do with our own health, lack of sleep, poor exercise, eating and work or relationship stressors. But please keep these out of toilet training, and do your best to solve these issues for your own health and peace of mind.

Children are very sensitive to their parent's mood, so you need to be very careful with your body language, sighs of exasperation, rolling of your eyes, frustrated looks, hurtful words etc. Above all do not yell, scold, snap or name call to your child when it comes to toilet training (or any behaviour for that matter) at home or out and about in public.

Do not use words like 'stinky bum' 'smelly' 'yucky' 'icky' 'bad' 'lazy' or phrases such as 'why can't you learn'. All these destroy a child's confidence and self-esteem. In fact it actually makes it harder for them to learn new skills. Toilet training is just another new skill and like all new skills some children pick it up quicker than others and they don't always get it right while learning.

You need patience in bucket loads and bucket loads to toilet train a toddler. Punishment will only make it more difficult and it will certainly take longer. If you are not in the right frame of mind as a parent, perhaps you should consider making some changes to your own life and waiting a little longer to start toilet training so that you are better able to be positive for your toddler.

SAVE IT FOR THE NAPPY

Often in my clinic parents ask about why their toddler is toilet trained with wees but refuses to sit on the potty to do a poo? They are preferring instead to hold on and wait until their nappy is put on at lunchtime for a sleep or asking for their nappy to be put on and only then doing a poo in their nappy.

The other common issue can be going and hiding in their bedroom and closing the door or going behind the rocking chair and doing their poo in their pants. All of these issues are fear based. A child who has had a fall or fright when using the toilet often develops this type of fear reaction. The answer to this problem is to address their fears and talk about the day that they got a fright, and how they now think it's scary, but that they actually are okay doing a poo because nothing will happen to them.

To address these types of issues you need a plan and steps to work on bit by bit. You base the steps on what is the next step closer you can get your child to sitting on the potty. This may take several months. You combine it with rewards, lots of positive praise and attention just for doing the next step. For example, the first step for a child that hides is to give them permission to use their nappy as you want the poos to come out. Children will hold for days and days out of fear. Then the first goal would be for them to move from behind their rocking chair where they hide to in the bedroom or in the hallway near the toilet. The plan you design is individual and takes into account your child's own fears. Keep thinking: "What can we do that is one step closer to where we need to be?" This can be solved, though I recommend you seek expert advice on this. If you leave it, the fears don't usually disappear. This is actually a type of fear based anxiety and a psychologist can help you work out the steps and plan of action.

SMEARING

Quite a lot of toddlers smear their poo, whether it is on the toilet wall or their bedroom wall. Why? Mostly due to curiosity and because they can. What to do? Make sure clothes at bedtime are more secure, think overalls, tricky clips etc, and putting nappies on backwards is also a great tip.

After your child has smeared, just be matter of fact and say, "Mummy doesn't like this, poos go into the toilet." My suggestion would also be to get your child to help clean it up if appropriate. They can certainly be given a wipe and instructed to clean it off the wall. Be careful that this doesn't become a game though!

If they smear while sitting on the toilet, then supervise them closely and give them something else to do while on the toilet: the potty watch is great, or have a few small books to look at.

STICKY BOTTOMS

Often with toilet training, our toddler's bottoms become sticky, parents don't like to discuss this with them but it's important that you do. Your toddler needs to learn to wipe their bottom and it really isn't that easy for them to learn.

So be patient and teach them to keep wiping until the toilet paper is clean. Show them how to pull off another section of toilet paper and to try again. When it is really sticky then the flushable wet toilet wipes are very handy. So keep a packet of them on the top of the toilet ready for use. Remember to wipe from front to back especially for girls. Show your toddler what to do and where to put the pants that have skid marks on them – my suggestion is a bucket in the laundry or bathroom.

TRYING EVERY TOILET

Once you start toilet training, toddlers suddenly find that there is a whole exciting world out there of new and different toilets all to be explored. So no sooner than have you arrived at a friend's house, or the café, or the shopping centre, it is quite normal for your toddler to declare 'that they need to go to the toilet'. Once you take them, go back to what you were initially doing. They are likely to ask again and again.

This is normal and this will pass in time. Firstly, think of it as a good sign that your toddler will know where the toilet is when they really do have to go. Secondly, they may be getting a few false starts with their body and thirdly, they are just really curious about toilets – it is better to be curious than to have a toddler who is sensitive and doesn't want to use any other toilet. In time this will settle, just patiently take them to the toilet yet again! All of these toilets are interesting and look different! The novelty will soon wear off and they will only go when they really need to.

If your toddler is very confident and suddenly takes off and goes to the bathroom by themselves – or announces that they are certain they can do it by themselves, please note your toddler is way too young to be going by themselves in a public bathroom, so an adult must get up and go and join them.

Disposable paper toilet seat covers for hygiene when out

Nicole's Tip:

It can be very handy when out and about to use disposable paper toilet covers for public toilets. It's a quick and hygienic way to use public toilets especially if you don't have time to do a thorough wipe with antibacterial wipes or sprays.

WHERE'S THE TOILET? OUT AND ABOUT

When going out, whether it be to the grocery shops, a park, a café, or a friend's house, make sure that your child knows where the toilet it as soon as you get there. Waiting until your child does the urgent announcement that they need to wee is generally disastrous and too late! Upon arriving, point it out to your child or if in a shopping centre, mentally work out in your head how far you are to the nearest toilet as most shopping centres have more than one.

Let your friends and family know that you are toilet training if you are with them or in their house and be prepared, either take your potty or check out their toilet. Show your toddler their potty to start with if you are taking it. Remember to select your toddler's clothes with care and make it easy for them to rush to the toilet and pull or lift their clothes.

Out and about make sure you know where the toilets are

WORKING MUMS AND DADS

If you are both working full time and your toddler is ready to start toilet training then I believe it's a good idea for one parent to take a week off work and devote it to toilet training. I can hear your protests now, but it really is worth it. Please consider this carefully.

If taking a week off work is just not possible then at least take a Monday off and start on a Saturday morning and give yourself three days at home to get a good start – have a long weekend. But sure to work with your daycare staff at the same time so that it is consistent when your toddler returns on the Tuesday.

Ask Nicole

DADS AND DAUGHTERS IN PUBLIC BATHROOMS

Question: When my husband is out at the shopping centre and my daughter needs to go to the toilet, what should he do? Can she go to the men's bathroom? Or should he ask someone else to take her into the women's?

Answer: Today most shopping centres or offices have parent bathrooms, where either parent feels comfortable taking their child in to use the toilet or to change a nappy. They are specially designed for this purpose. So if one is available go for this choice as usually there may be a line up in the women's or men's.

If there is no choice, then most dads simply take their daughter into the men's toilet. Lots of dads do so. They often just pick them up and carry them in and cradle them into their shoulder as they walk in past the urinal and go to the toilet stall that has a door, just in the same way that a mother does when she takes her son into the women's bathroom. This is quite okay and common to see. I would certainly avoid asking someone else to take your daughter into the women's toilet.

FEAR OF FLUSHING

Question: My toddler is afraid of the flushing of the toilet. How can I help her to get over this fear?

Answer: This is not unusual. I find more sensitive children can be quite interested in the toilet, the water and the hole, but when the toilet is flushed get a fright at the sound, the hole or simply just the concept of 'where does it all go?' Your daughter will get past this fear in time.
However, here are some great ideas that will help her fear.

- Ask her, "Will you flush or will I?"
- If she clearly doesn't want to and starts to get upset, ask her to start washing her hands and as she leaves the toilet room then flush the toilet.
- After a few days or longer, flush earlier and earlier in the process of her leaving. Talk to her or sing a song as you flush. This way you add a positive experience in order to diminish a negative experience. The psychological term for this is 'pairing'.
- Chat casually at other times about what happens when the toilet flushes
- Get a book from the library about plumbing or draw your own picture – toddlers love to learn.
- Make a game of it – stand a few feet from the toilet and toss in popcorn or cereal and flush them.

Perhaps choose special cereal and make that 'flush-only' or your toddler might start flushing all sorts of random things.

All these tips will slowly help her overcome her fear of flushing. Just don't make a big deal of it.

SHOCKED AT THEIR OWN POO

Question: We have started toilet training and it was going very well and yesterday my daughter saw her poo coming out and started screaming. Now she is terrified when she does a poo and clings onto me and cries hysterically. I'm not sure what to do now?

Answer: This is so very common, it is likely that your daughter was not expecting to do a poo and not aware of where is really comes from, so often when this happens toddlers get a fright and are scared about how this big thing is coming out of them. At this point you need to talk about how she got a fright, but how good it is to do a poo, and how good it is to do a poo on the potty. Demonstration and showing her mummy and daddy's poo will help as well.

If you are not progressing with these strategies and need to - it is okay to go back to putting a nappy on to do the poo and trying to get her to sit on the potty with her nappy on to do the poo. Then demonstrate by showing her how to tip the poo into the toilet saying, 'Our poo goes into the toilet' then wipe her and flush it away. The next step is then to undo the Velcro on the nappy and line the potty with the nappy to catch it. It's important that she doesn't start to 'hold' onto her poos and delay them coming out. I would also seek advice about this issue.

STALLING BEDTIME WITH TOILET VISITS

Question: Since we started potty training my son after I've tucked him into bed announces that 'he has to go to the toilet' again and again, now bedtime is dragging out. How do I know if he really has to go?

Answer: Your son has worked out that he is in a very powerful position, and that asking 'to go to the toilet' is the one phrase that makes a parent think twice and follow through on. He gets to delay bedtime. This is a very powerful position to be in and he uses it because it works. But you are right, what if.... He really does need to go to the toilet? Often there is for toddlers a need to go to the toilet once they have lay down in bed and their body has relaxed and their bladder then tells them that they really need to go. At the early stages of toilet training if he is going and saying this six times, then you need to bring it back to two at the most.

The first will be about 5-10 minutes after being put into the bed and then tell him firmly that he may get up and go to the toilet only once more so make sure that he really needs to go. When you do take him just be very matter of fact about going, take him, don't chat on the way, no stops for drinks of water or collecting the teddy that he forgot, and use little eye contact.

If he is really persistent in going and asking again and again, it's quite okay to put a spare potty in his bedroom, usually once this option is presented it is rarely ever used and has called the bluff!

TOUCHING HIS PENIS ON THE POTTY

Question: Often when I put my son on the potty he reaches down and plays with his penis! I'm not sure what to do about it and don't want him doing this?

Answer: Your son is just exploring his body parts, to him his penis is no different to any other interesting body part, and he suddenly has access to his penis when his nappy is off. He may have also worked out that it feels nice to touch it and it changes shape, there is nothing sexual about this it is just something new to play with. I understand your desire to not have him fiddle, so the answer to this is really distraction. Just give him a book to read while he sits and waits so that his hands are busy holding the book, or sing a song that has actions to it and get him to join in. Keep him busy.

Support – Have more questions to ask?

ONLINE SHOP AND SUPPORT PACKAGES:

I understand that as a parent you often have your own specific questions that you'd like answered, just need reassurance that you are heading in the right direction or may like a specific action plan of steps for your toddler. In response to this we have a range of support options for parents so you can ask questions, and get expert matter of fact answers that really work. Parents tell us this gives them confidence and relief to have their questions answered.

If you'd like to know more you can go to my website www.babysmiles.com.au/shop and you will find a number of different flexible options: whether it is email support for parenting questions, joining our membership and asking in our forum, skype, facetime or phone appointments or perhaps you would prefer to come into our clinic and meet me and ask your questions in your own consultation.

We are constantly adding to our range of services for parents so have a look on the website to get started. Not sure what you need? Please feel free to email us personally on info@babysmiles.com.au anytime.

Here is my Potty Training chart, a full A4 version can also be downloaded from my website.

BABYsmiles Potty Training Chart

	I said I needed to go potty	I pulled down my pant by myself	I Sat on the potty	I went did pee on the potty	I did a poo on the potty	I Stayed dry all day
Monday						
Tuesday						
Wednesday						
Thursday						
Friday						
Saturday						
Sunday						

Bristol Stool Chart

Type 1	Separate hard lumps, like nuts (hard to pass)
Type 2	Sausage-shaped but lumpy
Type 3	Like a sausage but with cracks on the surface
Type 4	Like a sausage or snake, smooth and soft
Type 5	Soft blobs with clear-cut edges
Type 6	Fluffy pieces with ragged edges, a mushy stool
Type 7	Watery, no solid pieces. Entirely Liquid

Bristol Stool chart can be downloaded from my website www.babysmiles.com.au

Type 4 is ideal – like as a usage. Type 1 & 2 your toddler is constipated Type 6 & 7 your toddler has diarrhoea

SIGNS YOUR TODDLER IS READY TO TOILET TRAIN

Child Readiness Checklist

- ☐ She can be dry for a couple of hours at a time
- ☐ Her poos are regular and you can see a pattern in the time of day
- ☐ She notices or gives you a clue that she is doing a poo or wee – usually toddlers stop what they are doing, crouch down or bends their knees, clutch their nappy area or sometimes even go and hide when she is doing a wee
- ☐ She simply tells you or asks to be changed after she has done a wee or poo
- ☐ She is keen to wear underwear or training pants
- ☐ She may look for a little privacy when doing a wee or poo
- ☐ She is able to follow simple directions like 'sit down', 'quick, let go'
- ☐ She wants to co- operate with mum giving instructions
- ☐ She can walk well – as she needs to actually be able to get to the toilet in a hurry
- ☐ She can pull pants up and down – she needs to be able to basically get dressed and undressed. We will make it easy though with clothing that is easy to remove while training, no need to make it trickier than it is!

- ☐ She has a basic understanding of what the toilet is for
- ☐ She wants to please mum or dad, and is not in the difficult 'no' stage as she wants to see what you will do about it..... You don't need any battles about toilet training!
- ☐ She can sit quietly for short periods of time say 5 – 10 minutes to do a puzzle, read a book? She will need to on the potty.
- ☐ She can tell you that she needs to go? Or notices she is doing a wee.

You don't need every one of these points on the readiness checklist to be present however your toddler needs MOST. The more that are there, the more successful toilet training will be for both of you.

Nicole's Tip:

If your child isn't 'ready' then it can be frustrating and discouraging. If in doubt? WAIT a little longer, read this list and think about it again. I suggest waiting 8 weeks then try again.

SIGNS YOU AS A PARENT ARE READY TO TOILET TRAIN YOUR TODDLER

Parent Readiness Checklist

Signs you – 'the parent' is ready

Your child is ready now what about you?

When you are teaching your child anything, especially toilet training you as the parent must be willing to do this, feeling pretty patient and keen to move onto the next stage. Positive, Positive and more Positive…

> If you are going through a difficult time emotionally, feel impatient with your child, are easily frustrated and tired then this is not the right time to start toilet training.

Toilet training is not done in a day, no matter the promises you've heard – it is usually weeks and then months before you are confident that your child is day trained.

Your job as a parent is like a coach. You need to help remind, be patient, teach new skills, clean up accidents without reprimand, wash dirty clothes, change clothes, help your toddler run to the toilet at a moment's notice – read, drop everything you are doing immediately and take your toddler, all the while being positive and encouraging them to hold on!

Make no mistake that this process can be frustrating at times and accidents will happen without a doubt. But if you prepare yourself and know how you are to approach this, then teach your child, pull ups will soon be a thing of the past.

PARENT READINESS CHECKLIST

- ☐ Am I positive?
- ☐ Do I have time?
- ☐ Am I getting enough sleep?
- ☐ Am I patient?
- ☐ Do I have all the things I need?
- ☐ Is this the right time for our family?

So your *child* is ready and so are *you*, positive attitude and enthusiasm at the ready? Well then, it's time...

STEP 1 – TOILET TRAINING 7 DAY CHART

MY POTTY CHART

STEP 1 – Trying and Learning - Put a sticker on as you sit and try! A small sticker for trying, a big sticker for a wee or poo in the potty

Monday	Tuesday	Wednesday	Thursday	Friday	Saturday	Sunday

www.babysmiles.com.au

Copyright Babysmiles

NICOLE PIEROTTI :: No More Nappies

STEP 2 – TOILET TRAINING 7 DAY CHART

STEP 3 – TOILET TRAINING 7 DAY CHART

PROFESSIONAL HELP

If you have questions or concerns about any aspect of toilet training or you are dealing with a toddler who is fearful, holding onto wee or poo or being really defiant, ask for help. Rather than wait and hope that your child will grow out of it. Sometimes all that is needed is one consultation with a professional who works in this area to give you a plan of action, or can answer all your questions and concerns with expert advice. So contact your doctor, psychologist or contact our clinic on info@babysmiles.com.au for more information.

ACKNOWLEDGEMENTS

The writing of this book is really a culmination of the last twenty years of my specialised work and learning as a psychologist with babies and toddlers and my work and learning as a parent.

The expectation of my first child started a range of questions on how to parent for my husband and I. We had clear ideas of what we desired for our baby and ourselves: a good night's sleep, enjoyment of being a parent, a well behaved child – just to name a few.

What quickly became apparent to us both was that there were very few strategies to get us on this path. The more I read the more I realised how much conflicting information there is on parenting. That quickly became confusing. Thus this was the start of this new focus in my life, firstly personally and then professionally.

Twenty years later and having worked with hundreds & thousands of parents and given them countless strategies. I've written at least 700 articles for various magazines, newspapers and media on parenting. At last, I have written this book on Toilet Training. This would have to be the most asked for book and question from parents in all my years, so finally here it is. It is my second book in my series of BabyCare, and is a very practical, easy to read book with all the steps you need to know for teaching your toddler about the toilet.

Of course a big 'Thank You' to all the parents and babies, toddlers and children I have had the joy to work with over many years, you have all contributed to my depth of knowledge. It's been a pleasure.

Nicole

Other books-DVD's in Nicole Pierotti's Babysmiles Series.

There is a range of Babycare Books and DVD's.

Book 1 *Babycare :: Caring for your baby :: Birth to 6 months*

DVD *Babycare :: Caring for your baby :: Birth to 6 months*

Look out for upcoming titles in this series:

(available from www.babysmiles.com.au)

Thank you, Isabella.

www.ingramcontent.com/pod-product-compliance
Lightning Source LLC
Chambersburg PA
CBHW040322300426
44112CB00020B/2838